Kaffe Fassett's
Simple Shapes Spectacular Quilts

23 Original Quilt Designs

KAFFE FASSETT
with LIZA PRIOR LUCY
Photographs by Debbie Patterson

STC Craft | A Melanie Falick Book | Stewart, Tabori & Chang, New York

This book is dedicated to all of the quilters worldwide who ask "Where do you get your ideas?"

Published in 2010 by Stewart, Tabori & Chang
An imprint of ABRAMS.

Library of Congress Cataloging-in-Publication Data

Fassett, Kaffe.
Simple shapes spectacular quilts / Kaffe Fassett with Liza Prior Lucy;
photography by Debbie Patterson.
   p. cm.
ISBN 978-1-58479-837-8
1. Patchwork. 2. Quilting. I. Lucy, Liza Prior. II. Title.
TT835.F3695 2010
746.46'041—dc22
    2009015803

Editors: Sally Harding and Melanie Falick
Designer: Anna Christian
Production Manager: Jacqueline Poirier

The text of this book was composed in Mrs. Eaves and Gotham.

Printed and bound in China
10 9 8 7 6 5 4 3 2

THE ART OF BOOKS SINCE 1949

115 West 18th Street
New York, NY 10011
www.abramsbooks.com

CONTENTS

SQUARES 10

Three patchwork designs that illustrate how easy it is to create lavish quilts with simple squares

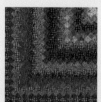

RECTANGLES 36

Four colorful quilts that celebrate the versatility and geometric simplicity of the basic brick and strip shapes

TRIANGLES 62

Four opulent patchworks composed entirely of basic triangles

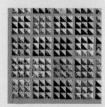

DIAMONDS 86

Five quilts made up of diamond patches cut from extravagantly patterned fabrics

QUARTER CIRCLES 126

Three quilts using quarter-circle geometry in an array of spectacular colors

CIRCLES 148

Four quilts featuring circle shapes to showcase opulent, vibrant color

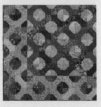
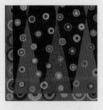

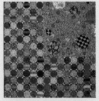

INTRODUCTION

On my way to teach a workshop in Switzerland I happened upon an amazing book called *Elements of Design* by Loan Oei and Cecile de Kegel. The version I saw was in German, so I couldn't read the text, but I was instantly drawn in and lit up by the handsome photographs of basic shapes found in nature and also echoed in manmade objects. It resonated with me, as I am always fascinated by the way basic squares, circles, and triangles can become the simple building blocks in designs of great richness and ingenuity.

Sometimes it is hard to find the simple geometry within an ornate piece of embroidery, architectural ornament, or woven rug. That's why I find quilts so exciting—your eye can suddenly catch the bare bones of a quilt's geometry even though it's buzzing with intertwining floral patterns. Even basic square patches all the same size can be used to create complex compositions. For example, just setting square patches "on point," so they look like fat diamonds, will give a quilt a totally different look than one in which the squares are presented in their standard orientation. And if the pattern and color in one square reaches out to relate to its neighbor, the square can become downright camouflaged, making the design even more intriguing. Squares that appear as squares and then merge into neighboring squares will make the geometric format go in and out of "focus" across the whole quilt so that the patches appear to move and dance.

My ambition in this book is to draw attention to the basic shapes that we cut for quilts as they appear in our surroundings. The more we spot these shapes in the world around us—particularly when we travel and our eye is so much fresher, picking up on all the details we usually miss—the more we can access the rich world of inspiration they provide. After all, we are so much more confident to attempt an idea if we have seen it laid out in real-life scenarios. For example, I become much more excited about using repetitions of stripes when I remember the fascinating stacks of mattresses with their varied tickings in an Indian market, or all of those

Here's a sampling of places to look for simple geometric shapes—in antique textiles, Islamic mosaics, garden landscapes, architecture—mixed in with a few of my quilt and needlepoint designs that sprang from such rich sources. A medley of colors and shapes are all around us—open your eyes and you will see them.

jaunty awning stripes on deck chairs in English parks. Tile floors and walls with bold repeats softened by the vagaries of glazes awaken me again to how satisfying squares can be.

It's always refreshing to the creative mind to pare everything back to the basics and start afresh. In the mid 1960s I embarked on a series of painted still lifes using only shades of white. It was a fast from the muddle of colors I'd been playing with since leaving art college. After a few years I cautiously introduced some delicately patterned china into my monochrome still lifes. Then I added embroidered or printed cloth in neutral or faded shades of color. Once those floodgates that kept any color from my work were breeched, it was only a matter of months before the full Oriental palette I love flooded onto my canvases.

Paring down to basic shapes did the same for my quilt designs. By starting from pure squares, triangles, diamonds, rectangles, circles, and quarter circles, my imagination soon ran riot, and here are the results. From now on, it will be a never-ending flow for me, as I hope it will be for you—to go on and on with simple shapes, constructing them into ever more ambitious structures. Working on this collection of quilts I wanted to recapture the totally absorbing time I had as a child creating toy villages from mill ends—triangles, oblongs, and squares of wood—my mother found at a lumberyard.

Because I am passing these ideas on to you to carry on with, I've tried to use formats that can be relayed in simple instructions and are easy to sew by machine. There are many quilts that are ideal for absolute beginners, such as Boston Common (pages 14 and 15) and Tilt (page 40), made entirely of simple squares or rectangles, respectively. Even one of my circles quilts, Floral Snowballs (page 153), is easy to stitch because the circles are created as an illusion by adding triangle corners to simple squares. If you'd like to sew a quilt by hand, consider my Stripescape (pages 44 and 45), a nice containable project. I had a ball stitching mine, using just two widths of strips cut from striped fabrics to create a very atmospheric landscape of earthy stripes.

When I went out to find locations for the quilts in this collection, my mind was totally engaged in a deeper way than it has been for any of my other collections. Suddenly, I wanted gritty industrial sites to show these arrangements of geometry. Bridges, building yards, abandoned houses, and tiled highway underpasses became fascinating to me. I discovered amazing settings within a two-mile radius of my north London home. One of these locations was an exciting old decaying bridge near Paddington with dark carved scrolls at each end. Another was a simple stack of car tires against a cobalt blue wall. But probably the most striking was a large modern ramp leading from a new housing project down to the parking area. The textured concrete walls of this ramp were ideal to show the wide range of quilt palettes for our title page, proving yet again how neutral gray is such a good foil to bring color to life. These backdrops were a refreshing change from the charm and pretty lushness I usually hunt for to show my quilts. Rusty surfaces and distressed, decaying walls became stunning to me. Ultimately, however, I couldn't resist a few more romantic locations that suited my quilts too well, like the bewitching north London cemetery with Victorian gothic memorials where I hung St. Marks (page 94).

Once you start on this sort of quest for geometric shapes, every stroll or ride you take can be studded with discoveries. While working on this book I walked with enthusiasm every weekend, making notes and taking snapshots of the basic shapes that I found in so many unexpected places.

I hope this book will help you start on your own stimulating search and design spree. Remember that my color recipes for the quilts that follow are just suggestions. Don't be afraid to take the plunge and choose a fresh color palette for each one. In keeping with the theme here, I hope you will look more closely at the world around you for inspiration in both color and shape. Add striking hues to simple shapes and you're sure to come up with your own original, spectacular quilts.

KAFFE Fassett

Although I chose mostly gritty industrial settings to showcase the quilts for this book, such as this London bridge (opposite page, top), I couldn't resist the occasional romantic backdrop like this mossy garden wall in Hampstead, London (opposite page, bottom).

The geometric inventiveness of Islamic mosaic (above) gives you an inkling of how simple shapes can be repeated and filled with color to create spectacular, energetic compositions that delight the eye.

SQUARES

The simple square is probably the most basic shape we see in everyday life, but what a paradox the square is. As I was hitting my stride in the 1950s, fresh out of art college, the saying went, "Be there or be square"—a harsh judgment on one's possible ordinariness. Yet as a design element that crops up in every aspect of our lives, squares are the basis of much that is richly inventive. I think of the classic decoration on Greek revival architecture that was so pervasive on establishment buildings as I was growing up in San Francisco. Great bronze doors studded with square shapes were one example I often noticed on banks and insurance buildings. In the 1960s, black-and-white checkerboard floors were all the rage in many upscale shops and domestic interiors in California; of course, now they are considered quite ordinary.

Later I would be lucky enough to travel far and wide and, of course, I saw squares everywhere. When I first traveled to Paris, I remember the thrill of seeing, in person, those simple red-and-white gingham tablecloths in all the bistros. In Japan, there were the big bold squares of moss checkerboarded with cut stone in gardens, and in India, one of the world's most pattern-obsessed countries, I was delighted to see painted and carved lattice grids of squares framing flowers, animals, and pottery motifs on the walls of old palaces. While making a film about color in Vietnam, I stumbled upon the best uses of squares I've ever seen. We were in a market in the northern city of Hanoi, in a saw-blade shop, when I spotted shiny square boxes of screws and nails in every size imaginable sparkling like sequins on an evening gown.

During a fascinating trip to South Africa, I once visited a stunning town completely painted by Ndebele women in gorgeous colorful geometry. Upon my arrival, the most famous of the women there announced with great power, "I am Ester, art woman!" Of course, the Africans present us with an endless variety of squares, not only in the ways in which they decorate their houses but also in their Kuba embroidery, batiks, tie-dyes, and mud cloths.

But you don't have to travel far for inspiration. In the West, every city has its skyscrapers, cold steel and glass surfaces made a little more human with their grids of square windows interrupting their vertical rise. On the outskirts of big cities my hungry eye is always on the lookout for huge yards of boxcars in rich reds, blues, and oranges next to railways, often the most colorful vision around.

Probably the single most inspiring uses of squares for me are decorative tiles, particularly those in Spain, Mexico, and Holland. I love how tiles decorate—and bring to life—so many otherwise ordinary spaces there. Risers on stairs, hallways, and courtyards are made magical with decorated tiles. Back in London, many hotels and pubs still glow with amber, maroon, and deep green tiles from the Victorian era, adding richness to their neighborhoods (the subtle differences in their glazes can light me up on a gray day). See a great example of some on the bottom right-hand corner of page 10.

In my knitting, I often resort to simple square formats to carry complexities of color. In quilting, squares are the most basic building blocks. They are the easiest of shapes to cut and sew, and they can be combined to make straightforward checkerboards in solid-colored fabrics or they can be made with highly patterned fabrics so that each square converses with its neighbor. They can be tied in the corners with bright, fluffy threads or placed on point, each one standing on one of its corners (how different the square looks this way!). They can all be the same size or different sizes. Close your eyes and think creatively about the square and a whole new set of possibilities arises, as you will see in this chapter, and also in a few quilts in other chapters: Clay Tiles (page 67) is composed of triangle-studded squares; Damask Quarters (page 130) is all squares with quarter circles; and Earthy Mitered Boxes (page 69) relies on four triangles stitched together to create squares of three different scales.

The primitive window treatment on this Japanese country house shows a playful use of simple squares (opposite page, top) that would translate easily into a patchwork format. Closer to home, everything on the façade of this English building (opposite page, bottom) attracts me: the distressed stones, patterned curtains, and metal window grids. But best of all are the changing glaze tones on the lively tile panel. Spring Boston Common (above) shows how the atmosphere of this tile panel can be captured in squares of patterned fabric.

◀ AUTUMN BOSTON COMMON

The melting and merging and dramatic changes of pace in this patchwork layout have always fascinated me. For this version, I picked all the spotty, dotty fabrics in my collection and arranged them so they nearly merge with each other from row to row (see close-up above right). I have also seen this quilt layout done with white background fabrics among more tonal prints or with more contrasting prints and daring color changes, both ideas that I'd like to try. We drove to a tiny village in north Wales to shoot the quilt on a beautifully patinated doorway.

See instructions on pages 20–25.

◀ SPRING BOSTON COMMON

When I finished Autumn Boston Common, I suddenly wanted a lighter cheery mood, and since I had many of the same dotty fabrics in brighter colorways, I used those to create this fresh breath of spring.

I love the way these spring colors respond to the yellow background of the shopfront (just down the road from my house) where we photographed it. The fresh pastel tones make me think of rows of tulips in Dutch fields in the spring. Boston Common could also be done quite graphically with polka dots in different scales and colors.

See instructions on pages 20–25.

STRIPED DONUT

Striped Donut was inspired by a photo of a vintage quilt made with florals and solids and, most memorable to me, a few bold stripes. The strong diagonal of the original was enhanced by the solid bright centers of each bow-tie donut shape, and some of the solids were dark blue and black so the centers became a sharp, sequinlike accent that really carried the eye up the diagonal. The soft dusty palette with the occasional strong dark stripe that I chose for my version reflects the mood I was in at the time that I designed it. You might want to take your inspiration from African Kuba fabrics and do the whole quilt in browns, golds, and ocher stripes, which would make a great masculine statement. This layout and approach would also be exciting for the black and white fans of this world, perhaps with scarlet, magenta, and dark pink centers.

See instructions on pages 26–30.

YELLOW POTPOURRI

The secret to this quilt's success is seeking out the largest florals on the market. Leaf prints and bold stripes and geometrics can be used to good effect as well. I used to advise quilters to stick to a strong color bias in medium to light color tones—in other words, to minimize the contrast. Now, after some years of leading workshops on this design, I've seen that more contrast, if done with flair and a good color eye, can be wonderful. So my advice now is to start toward a color bias— say golden ochers or pinks and oranges—and collect every large print you can find. If a turquoise or cobalt blue added in seems to work in a strange way, try it.

I love yellows, so it was inevitable I'd go for a yellow version of this great layout. Bright pinks, lavenders, lime, and sky blues always seem to enhance yellow, so those crept in. I went for some deep ochers and orangey golds, but mostly I tried for a luminous glow of lemon yellowness. I fussy-cut some of my florals, centering a single bloom in the patch, to accentuate the flower faces. This is particularly punchy to do on the medium and smallest blocks where you can bull's-eye a flower center and really give the whole work a more articulate, considered feel.

See instructions on pages 31-35.

BOSTON COMMON

This is a perfect quilt for a beginner. It is made almost entirely of square patches, with triangle patches only around the outer edge. The squares are set "on point"—the corners of the squares point upward and downward and side to side. Use one of these two colorways in Kaffe Fassett and Rowan fabrics or create a unique one of your own.

FINISHED SIZE

Autumn Boston Common
96" × 99 1/2" (244 cm × 253 cm)

Spring Boston Common
78 1/4" × 82" (199 cm × 208 cm)

MATERIALS

Autumn Boston Common (shown on opposite page): Use cotton quilting fabrics 44–45" (112–114 cm) wide

Spring Boston Common (shown on page 15): Use cotton quilting fabrics 44–45" (112–114 cm) wide

PATCHWORK FABRICS

Autumn Boston Common: An assortment of 17 different medium-scale dotty and circular motif prints in autumnal colors (predominantly reds and greens, with brownish accents) in the amounts listed for the 17 fabrics below—OR the following 17 Kaffe Fassett fabrics:

Fabric A: 1/2 yd (46 cm) *Paperweight* in Algae
Fabric B: 1/8 yd (12 cm) *Organic Dot* in Spring
Fabric C: 1/8 yd (12 cm) *Organic Dot* in Contrast
Fabric D: 1/4 yd (25 cm) *Paperweight* in Pumpkin
Fabric E: 3/4 yd (70 cm) *Organic Dot* in Gold
Fabric F: 3/4 yd (70 cm) *Roman Glass* in Byzantine
Fabric G: 3/4 yd (70 cm) *Auricula* in Black

Fabric H: 1 yd (92 cm) *Auricula* in Red
Fabric I: 1 yd (92 cm) *Dahlia Bloom* in Autumn
Fabric J: 1/3 yd (31 cm) *Dahlia Bloom* in Succulent
Fabric K: 1 yd (92 cm) *Auricula* in Green
Fabric L: 1 yd (92 cm) *Organic Dot* in Brown
Fabric M: 1 yd (92 cm) *Roman Glass* in Jungle
Fabric N: 1 yd (92 cm) *Paperweight* in Gypsy
Fabric O: 1/2 yd (46 cm) *Paperweight* in Paprika
Fabric P: 1 1/4 yd (1.2 m) *Auricula* in Olive
Fabric Q: 3/4 yd (70 cm) *Dahlia Bloom* in Lush

Spring Boston Common: An assortment of 17 different medium-scale dotty and circular motif prints, plus some subtle stripes in spring colors (predominantly blue-greens, with lime, orange, and red accents) in the amounts listed for the 17 fabrics below—OR the following 17 Kaffe Fassett and Rowan fabrics:

Fabric A: 1/2 yd (46 cm) *Fan Flower* in California
Fabric B: 1/8 yd (12 cm) *Organic Dot* in Mint
Fabric C: 1/2 yd (46 cm) *Tree Rings* in Purple
Fabric D: 1/4 yd (25 cm) *Guinea Flower* in Yellow
Fabric E: 3/4 yd (70 cm) *Diagonal Poppy* in Lavender
Fabric F: 3/4 yd (70 cm) *Dahlia Bloom* in Vintage
Fabric G: 1/2 yd (46 cm) *Spools* in Lavender

Fabric H: 1/4 yd (25 cm) *Dahlia Bloom* in Spring
Fabric I: 3/4 yd (70 cm) *Spools* in Jade
Fabric J: 1 yd (92 cm) *Diagonal Poppy* in Duck Egg
Fabric K: 1/2 yd (46 cm) *Guinea Flower* in Green
Fabric L: 1/2 yd (46 cm) *Shirt Stripes* in Soft
Fabric M: 1/2 yd (46 cm) *Jungle Paisley* in Grey
Fabric N: 1/2 yd (46 cm) *Fan Flower* in Red
Fabric O: 3/4 yd (70 cm) *Cloisonné* in Aqua
Fabric P: 3/4 yd (70 cm) *Rootlets* in Blue
Fabric Q: 1/2 yd (46 cm) *Guinea Flower* in Pink

OTHER INGREDIENTS

Backing fabric: 8 1/2 yd (7.8 m) of desired fabric for Autumn Boston Common; 5 yd (4.6 m) of desired fabric for Spring Boston Common

Binding fabric: 3/4 yd (70 cm) of a stripe

Cotton batting: 103" × 106" (260 cm × 270 cm) for Autumn Boston Common; 86" × 89" (215 cm × 225 cm) for Spring Boston Common

Quilting thread: Green thread for Autumn Boston Common; pink thread for Spring Boston Common

Templates: Use templates C, D, and E (see pages 182 and 183)

Autumn Boston Common Assembly

KEY

Fabric A   Fabric C   Fabric E   Fabric G   Fabric I   Fabric K   Fabric M   Fabric O   Fabric Q

Fabric B   Fabric D   Fabric F   Fabric H   Fabric J   Fabric L   Fabric N   Fabric P

AUTUMN BOSTON COMMON

CUTTING PATCHES

Cut the number of square patches from each fabric as listed below, then follow the Rings Table when arranging the rings of squares around the two center squares.

1,458 squares: Cut template-C squares as follows:

44 from fabric A, 6 from fabric B, 10 from fabric C, 14 from fabric D, 88 from fabric E, 100 from fabric F, 80 from fabric G, 116 from fabric H, 132 from fabric I, 38 from fabric J, 152 from fabric K, 152 from fabric L, 58 from fabric M, 144 from fabric N, 66 from fabric O, 168 from fabric P, and 90 from fabric Q.

106 large edge triangles: Cut 106 template-D triangles from fabric M.

4 small corner triangles: Cut four template-E triangles from fabric M.

ASSEMBLING TOP

Arrange the patches as shown on the assembly diagram on page 22, either laying them out on the floor or sticking them to a cotton-flannel design wall. Start the arrangement at the center with the two fabric-A squares, and add the rings of color one by one outward (see the Rings Table).

Using the seam allowance marked on the templates throughout, sew the squares (and edge triangles) together in diagonal rows as shown on the assembly diagram. Then sew the diagonal rows together.

FINISHING QUILT

Press the quilt top. Layer the quilt top, batting, and backing, then baste the layers together (see page 181).

Using green thread, machine-quilt meandering circular shapes over the quilt.

Trim the quilt edges. Then cut the binding fabric on the bias and sew it on around the edge of the quilt (see page 181).

Rings Table for Autumn Boston Common

This table gives the color sequence, starting from the center of the quilt, of the 26 rings of squares around the two center squares on the quilt.

2 Center Squares	Fabric A
Ring 1 (6 squares)	Fabric B
Ring 2 (10 squares)	Fabric C
Ring 3 (14 squares)	Fabric D
Ring 4 (18 squares)	Fabric E
Ring 5 (22 squares)	Fabric F
Ring 6 (26 squares)	Fabric G
Ring 7 (30 squares)	Fabric H
Ring 8 (34 squares)	Fabric I
Ring 9 (38 squares)	Fabric J
Ring 10 (42 squares)	Fabric A
Ring 11 (46 squares)	Fabric K
Ring 12 (50 squares)	Fabric L
Ring 13 (54 squares)	Fabric G
Ring 14 (58 squares)	Fabric M
Ring 15 (62 squares)	Fabric N
Ring 16 (66 squares)	Fabric O
Ring 17 (70 squares)	Fabric E
Ring 18 (74 squares)	Fabric P
Ring 19 (78 squares)	Fabric F
Ring 20 (82 squares)	Fabric N
Ring 21 (86 squares)	Fabric H
Ring 22 (90 squares)	Fabric Q
Ring 23 (94 squares)	Fabric P
Ring 24 (98 squares)	Fabric I
Ring 25 (102 squares)	Fabric L
Ring 26 (106 squares)	Fabric K
Edge Triangles	Fabric M

Spring Boston Common Assembly

KEY

■ Fabric A   ■ Fabric C   ■ Fabric E   ■ Fabric G   ■ Fabric I   ■ Fabric K   ■ Fabric M   ■ Fabric O   ■ Fabric Q

■ Fabric B   ■ Fabric D   ■ Fabric F   ■ Fabric H   ■ Fabric J   ■ Fabric L   ■ Fabric N   ■ Fabric P

SPRING BOSTON COMMON

CUTTING PATCHES

Cut the number of square patches from each fabric as listed below, then follow the Rings Table when arranging the rings of squares around the two center squares.

968 squares: Cut template-C squares as follows:

68 from fabric A, 6 from fabric B, 45 from fabric C, 14 from fabric D, 80 from fabric E, 76 from fabric F, 61 from fabric G, 30 from fabric H, 108 from fabric I, 124 from fabric J, 42 from fabric K, 46 from fabric L, 50 from fabric M, 58 from fabric N, 78 from fabric O, and 82 from fabric P.

86 large edge triangles: Cut 86 template-D triangles from fabric Q.

4 small corner triangles: Cut four template-E triangles from fabric Q.

ASSEMBLING TOP

Arrange the patches as shown on the assembly diagram at left, either laying them out on the floor or sticking them to a cotton-flannel design wall. Start the arrangement at the center with the two fabric-A squares, and add the rings of color one by one outward (see the Rings Table).

Using the seam allowance marked on the templates throughout, sew the squares (and edge triangles) together in diagonal rows as shown on the assembly diagram. Then sew the diagonal rows together.

FINISHING QUILT

Press the quilt top. Layer the quilt top, batting, and backing, then baste the layers together (see page 181).

Using pink thread, machine-quilt meandering flower shapes over the quilt.

Trim the quilt edges. Then cut the binding fabric on the bias and sew it on around the edge of the quilt (see page 181).

Rings Table for Spring Boston Common

This table gives the color sequence, starting from the center of the quilt, of the 21 rings of squares around the two center squares on the quilt.

2 Center Squares	Fabric A
Ring 1 (6 squares)	Fabric B
Ring 2 (10 squares)	Fabric C
Ring 3 (14 squares)	Fabric D
Ring 4 (18 squares)	Fabric E
Ring 5 (22 squares)	Fabric F
Ring 6 (26 squares)	Fabric G
Ring 7 (30 squares)	Fabric H
Ring 8 (34 squares)	Fabric I
Ring 9 (38 squares)	Fabric J
Ring 10 (42 squares)	Fabric K
Ring 11 (46 squares)	Fabric L
Ring 12 (50 squares)	Fabric M
Ring 13 (54 squares)	Fabric F
Ring 14 (58 squares)	Fabric N
Ring 15 (62 squares)	Fabric E
Ring 16 (66 squares)	Fabric A
Ring 17 (70 squares)	Fabrics C and G
Ring 18 (74 squares)	Fabric I
Ring 19 (78 squares)	Fabric O
Ring 20 (82 squares)	Fabric P
Ring 21 (86 squares)	Fabric J
Edge Triangles	Fabric Q

STRIPED DONUT

To achieve the effect of the donut shapes on this quilt, choose fabrics that have a combination of broad and narrow stripes. The mixture of the thick and thin stripes on the patches makes the donuts appear almost three-dimensional. Woven and printed stripes work equally well.

FINISHED SIZE
63" × 77" (160 cm × 195.5 cm)

MATERIALS
Use quilting cotton 44–45" (112–114 cm) wide

PATCHWORK FABRICS

Fabric A (stripes): 1/2–3/4 yd (46–70 cm) each of at least 14 different predominantly medium-toned multicolored woven and printed striped fabrics (each with a mixture of broad and narrow stripe widths) in a dusky palette of gray-greens, magentas, golds, rose pinks, oranges, reds, aquas, and grays (a few of the stripe fabrics should have black in them for a stark contrast); a total of approximately 7 yd (6.4 m)

Fabric B (solids): 3/4 yd (70 cm) each of six different solid-colored fabrics in light pumpkin orange, light pink, light green, lavender, light aqua blue, and coral—OR 3/4 yd (70 cm) each of the following six Kaffe Fassett fabrics:

Shot Cotton in Sunshine, Rosy, Apple, Lavender, Duck Egg, and Watermelon

Fabric C (border fabrics): 1/2 yd (46 cm) each of two different but similar striped fabrics (each with a mixture of broad and narrow stripe widths)

OTHER INGREDIENTS

Backing fabric: 4 1/2 yd (4.1 m) of desired fabric

Binding fabric: 3/4 yd (70 cm) of a stripe

Cotton batting: 70" × 84" (175 cm × 210 cm)

Quilting thread: Greenish gray thread

Templates: Use templates AA, BB, CC, DD, EE, and FF (see page 183)

CUTTING PATCHES

Cut the patches for the quilt center before cutting the border patches. Avoid cutting exact duplicates from the stripe fabric for each donut, as the liveliness of the arrangement is achieved by misaligning each ring of stripes.

QUILT CENTER

The blocks that make up the quilt center are arranged so that matching blocks form diagonal rows across the quilt as shown on the assembly diagram (page 29). Starting at the upper left corner of the quilt center, count the diagonal rows of matching blocks—the first diagonal row has a single block (the corner block), the second diagonal row two blocks, the third diagonal row three blocks, and so on, ending with the seventeenth row, which has again a single block (the corner block). Cut the patches for each diagonal row separately, and change the color theme in each diagonal row so that they will contrast with each other.

Diagonal row 1 (one block): Cut four template-AA patches from the same fabric A, aligning the stripes with the grain-line marker (the arrow), but not attempting to make each piece identical—the stripes should not line up exactly when the block is sewn together. Then cut six small template-BB triangles from the same solid-colored fabric B.

Diagonal row 2 (two blocks): Cut enough patches for two blocks—*for each of the two blocks*, cut four template-AA patches from the same fabric A (as explained for the first block) and six small template-BB triangles from the same solid-colored fabric B.

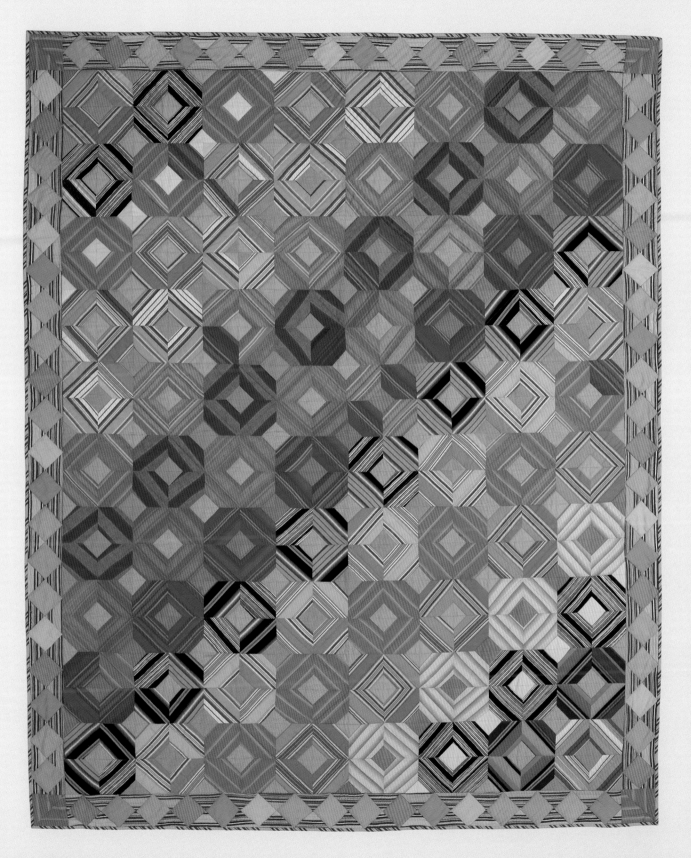

Concentric squares made from stripes is a compelling theme in Striped Donut. One of the most effective versions I've seen of the same simple geometry is the surface of this old paneled door. Here the distressed coloring of sky blues and warm ochery reds hums, and the carved lines add extra dimension. What a fabulous inspiration for a quilt! Made with ikat fabrics and hand-painted washy tones, it could be a winner.

Diagonal rows 3–17: Continue in this way, cutting pieces from the same stripe fabric and the same solid-colored fabric for each diagonal row of blocks. Diagonal row 3 has three blocks; diagonal row 4 has four blocks; diagonal row 5 has five blocks; diagonal row 6 has six blocks; diagonal row 7 has seven blocks; diagonal rows 8, 9, and 10 each have eight blocks; diagonal row 11 has seven blocks; diagonal row 12 has six blocks; diagonal row 13 has five blocks; diagonal row 14 has four blocks; diagonal row 15 has three blocks; diagonal row 16 has two blocks; and diagonal row 17 (the corner block) has one block.

Remaining small template-BB squares: Once you have made up the blocks and arranged them all for the quilt center, you will need to cut more small template-BB squares to fill in the missing corners on the blocks—but you can't do this until the arrangement is final and you can see which solid-colored fabric to use to match to the adjacent block.

BORDERS

72 squares: From fabric B (solid-colored fabric), cut a total of 72 template-CC squares, cutting about the same number from each of the six colors.

136 medium-size border triangles: From each fabric C, cut 68 template-DD triangles, aligning the stripes with the grain-line marker—for a total of 136 striped triangles.

16 small border triangles: From each fabric C, cut four template-EE triangles and four template-EE-reverse triangles, aligning the stripes with the grain-line marker—for a total of 16 triangles.

8 large corner triangles: From a single fabric A, cut four template-FF triangles and four template-FF-reverse triangles, aligning the stripes with the grain-line marker.

MAKING BLOCKS

Using the seam allowance marked on the templates, sew together the blocks.

80 blocks: Using the patches cut for each block (four matching template-AA pieces and six matching small template-BB triangles), sew together the block as shown in the block diagram in steps 1 and 2.

Striped Donut Block

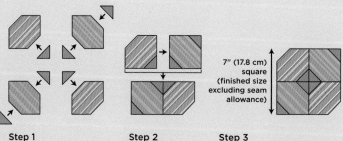

7" (17.8 cm) square (finished size excluding seam allowance)

Step 1
Sew on six small triangles.

Step 2
Sew together patches.

Step 3
Arrange the blocks in diagonal rows before sewing on missing corners.

Step 4
Determine the correct colors for the missing corners, then sew them on.

Striped Donut Assembly

KEY

Fabric A   Fabric B   Fabric C

Bold stripes create quite a different look for the bow-tie patch format. The border worked out particularly well on this quilt. I used the same colors for the bow-tie block centers and the on-point squares of the border and good medium stripes for their background. There is no need to cut the stripe fabrics exactly on the straight grain because a little off-grain cutting adds to the visual excitement of the composition.

When all the blocks are complete except for two missing corners as shown in step 3, you are ready to assemble the quilt top.

ASSEMBLING TOP

Arrange the quilt center as shown on the assembly diagram (page 29), either laying out the patches on the floor or sticking them to a cotton-flannel design wall. Arrange the matching blocks in diagonal rows.

Once the blocks are arranged, determine which solid-colored fabric (fabric B) to use for each of the two missing corners on each block—they should match the corners they touch on the adjacent rows. Cut out and sew on all the missing template-BB corners, but be careful to replace each block in the arrangement as you sew on the corners.

Using the seam allowance marked on the templates throughout, sew the blocks together in 10 horizontal rows of eight blocks each as shown on the assembly diagram. Then sew the 10 horizontal rows together.

Arrange the pieces for the side and top borders as shown on the assembly diagram, using 20 solid-colored squares for each side border and 16 for the top and bottom borders. Sew the small striped triangles, the medium-size striped triangles, and the solid squares together to form the borders.

For each of the four corner squares, sew together one large template-FF triangle and one large template-FF-reverse triangle so that the stripes meet at right angles. Sew one pieced corner square to each end of the top and bottom borders.

Sew the side borders to the quilt center, then sew on the top and bottom borders.

FINISHING QUILT

Press the quilt top. Layer the quilt top, batting, and backing, then baste the layers together (see page 181).

Using greenish gray thread, stitch-in-the-ditch around all the patches. Then machine-quilt a straight line through the center of each template-AA patch following the direction of the stripe. Next machine-quilt spaced lines across the triangle border patches parallel to the stripes.

Trim the quilt edges. Then cut the binding fabric on the bias and sew it on around the edge of the quilt (see page 181).

YELLOW POTPOURRI

This square-patch quilt is a good choice for a novice quilter because there aren't any set-in or angled seams. If you want to achieve a color wash like mine, make sure your fabric choices do not contrast wildly in lightness/darkness.

FINISHED SIZE

69″ × 102″ (184 cm × 272 cm)

MATERIALS

Use quilting cottons 44–45″ (112–114 cm) wide

PATCHWORK FABRICS

Main fabric (for square patches):
1/4–1 yd (46–92 cm) each of at least 15 different light-toned and medium-toned medium-scale and large-scale floral and vegetable prints in lemon yellows, bright pinks, lavenders, lime, deep ochers, orangey golds, and sky blues; a total of approximately 10–12 yd (9.2–11 m)

Inner-border fabric: 1/2 yd (46 cm) of a medium-scale floral print with pink, purple, and lavender flowers and ocher leaves on a light turquoise ground

OTHER INGREDIENTS

Backing fabric: 6 yd (5.6 m) of desired fabric

Binding fabric: 3/4 yd (70 cm) of one of the medium-scale floral prints used for the main fabric

Cotton batting: 76″ × 109″ (200 cm × 290 cm)

Quilting thread: Golden yellow thread

SPECIAL FABRIC NOTE

Because many of the patches are fussy-cut—cut with the motifs framed attractively within the patch—you need a little more fabric than is usual for a quilt this size. When purchasing the fabrics for the square patches, buy 1-yd (92-cm) lengths of the large-scale prints. For the medium-scale prints, 1/2 yd (46 cm) will be enough. If you are using a medium-scale print only for some of the smallest squares, buy 1/4-yd (25-cm) lengths.

CUTTING PATCHES

Fussy-cut most of the patches, carefully framing the floral motifs inside the patch shape.

QUILT CENTER

20 large squares: Cut 20 patches 9 1/2″ (25.5 cm) square from the main fabric.

53 medium-size squares: Cut 53 patches 6 1/2″ (17.5 cm) square from the main fabric.

130 small squares: Cut 130 patches 3 1/2″ (9.5 cm) square from the main fabric.

INNER BORDER

4 border strips: From the inner-border fabric, cut two strips 2″ × 87 1/2″ (5.5 cm × 233.5 cm) for the side borders; then cut two strips 2″ × 57 1/2″ (5.5 cm × 153.5 cm) for the top and bottom borders. (To make long enough strips, cut the strips selvage to selvage and sew together end to end.)

OUTER BORDER

When cutting "matching" patches for the outer border, cut the patches so they look similar but not necessarily identical.

4 corner patches: Cut four matching patches 6 1/2″ (17.5 cm) square from one of the main fabrics (a medium-scale print was used on this quilt).

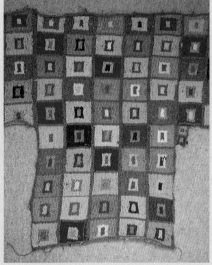

It's fun finding simple squares in so many corners of our lives. Here we have a rough-cut stone wall with lovely subtle variations of tone, and below it a knitted sample I did using bold squares with outlined centers. Both could be interpreted wonderfully into patchwork. The mortar between the stones and the fine gray grid in the knitted piece suggest how a very narrow sashing can be an interesting design element. If you try adding sashing to get this effect, be sure to keep it skinny. Too many quilts feature very wide sashings that take away from the beauty of the block arrangements.

4 center-border patches: Cut four matching patches 6 1/2" (17.5 cm) square from one of the main fabrics, using a different fabric than the one used for the corner patches.

28 patches for side borders: Cut seven sets of four matching patches 6 1/2" (17.5 cm) square, using a different one of the main fabrics for each set.

16 patches for top and bottom border: Cut three sets of four matching patches 6 1/2" (17.5 cm) square, using a different one of the main fabrics for each set. Then cut four matching patches 6 1/2" × 8" (17.5 cm × 21.5 cm) from another of the main fabrics.

ASSEMBLING TOP

Take your time arranging the patches of the center quilt—this is the fun part. Sprinkle the different fabrics randomly across the quilt and make sure that patches cut from the same fabric are not touching each other.

ARRANGING QUILT CENTER

Arrange the center of the quilt in three long panels as shown on the assembly diagram (page 34), either laying out the patches on the floor or sticking them to a cotton-flannel design wall.

ARRANGING OUTER BORDER

Next arrange the outer border around the edge of the quilt center, leaving a gap where the inner border will go. Position one corner patch at each corner of the quilt, and one center-border patch at the center of each side edge of the quilt and at the center of the top and bottom.

Divide the 28 patches cut for the side borders into two matching sets. Then arrange the patches for one of the side borders, positioning matching pairs radiating out from the center square so that each end of the border is a mirror of the other end. Arrange the other side border to match the first.

Divide the 16 patches cut for the top and bottom border into two matching sets. Then arrange the patches for the top border, positioning matching pairs radiating out from the center square so that each end of the border is a mirror of the other end; position the two longer patches at each end of this border, right before the corner patches. Arrange the bottom border to match the top.

SEWING PATCHES TOGETHER

Using a 1/4" (7.5 mm) seam allowance throughout, sew together the patches for the quilt center. First, sew the patches into three panels as shown on the assembly diagram. For each panel, sew the patches together in sections and then sew the sections together. The bold outlines on the diagram show how to divide each panel into sections and avoid having to use inset seams.

After the panels have been stitched together, sew the panels together.

Stitch the four inner border strips to the quilt center, sewing on the side strips first and then the top and bottom strips.

Yellow Potpourri Assembly

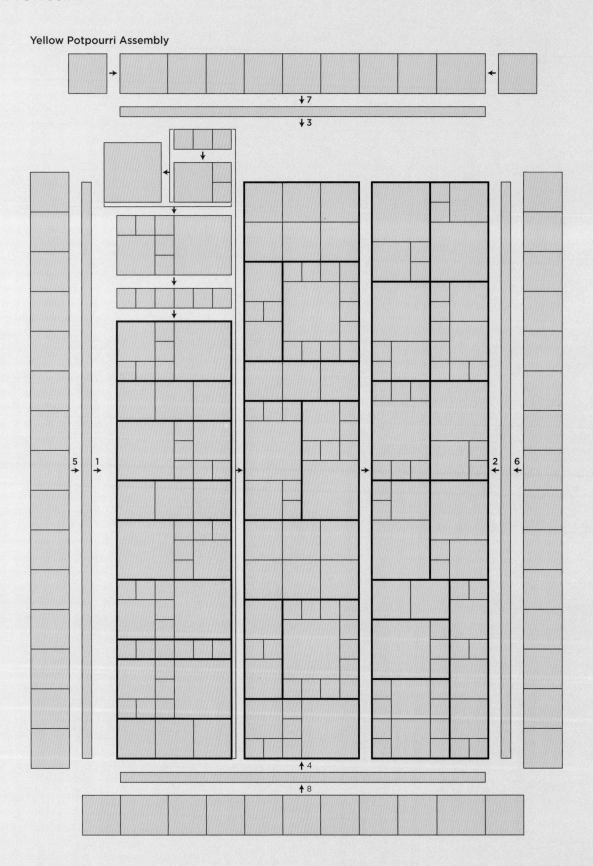

Sew together the 15 patches for each side border, then sew these to the quilt.

Sew together the nine patches for the top outer border and stitch a corner patch to each end. Sew together the patches for the bottom outer border in the same way. Then sew these borders to the quilt.

FINISHING QUILT

Press the quilt top. Layer the quilt top, batting, and backing, then baste the layers together (see page 181).

Machine-quilt around the outer edge of the biggest single flowers framed in each patch to emphasize them. Then machine-quilt meandering lines over the rest of the quilt.

Trim the quilt edges. Then cut the binding fabric on the bias and sew it on around the edge of the quilt (see page 181).

My passion for yellow started at a performance of the Peking Opera in which a huge painted yellow dragon dominated the stage, and the performers in front of the dragon wore shades of yellow with high pastel details. Here I've taken every flower print in yellow or sharp pastel tones in my range of fabrics and pieced them together for this confection of a quilt. The yellow brick wall intensifies its colors.

RECTANGLES

Rectangles are only second to squares in their pervasiveness around us. Brick walls, for a start, are everywhere as inspiration for simple rectangular shapes, most inspiring when they are laid out in quirky or playful ways. Walking around London, I'm always attracted by brick arches, bricks around window frames, and bricks arranged in diamond motifs on Victorian buildings (and even some new ones). I can even get excited when I see bricks stacked in an unusual way in building yards. Rectangles that are staggered are even called "bricks" in patchwork. One of the best of these I found on a porcelain buddha in the Victoria and Albert Museum in London (see page 36, bottom left). How jaunty the bright colors of his robe look in that simple geometric format, particularly contrasting with his flowery undergarment.

In the course of my life I get the chance to travel to many developing countries where I'm always visually inspired by the shanty towns on the fringes of large cities. When people are living on their wits, because of very low or nonexistent wages, they get especially inventive with whatever materials they can scavenge to create homes. The scrap dwellings in South Africa, Mexico, and India are like works of art to me. Rusty rectangular sheets of corrugated metal painted odd colors overlap to create patchwork houses. My travels in the United States provide me with inspiration as well. I have seen wonderful kitsch uses of multicolored, rectangular tar papers and license plates covering houses in obsessive decoration. This sort of naïve overkill is such a delight in the bland orderliness of suburban America.

Even if you don't have the chance to travel widely, it's possible to see so much of the world through books. In *The Way We Live* by Stafford Cliff and Gilles De Chabaneix, I was beguiled by a photo of a building in Bangkok made of weathered, rectangular planks of wood spiced with sky blue, pink, and mint green boards scavenged from different-colored buildings. I was so inspired by the random layout of colors that I created Stripescape (page 44) in response.

I think the most spectacular use of rectangles I have ever seen is the vast mosque in Cordoba, Spain. As you step through the door, as far as you can see there is a forest of pillars that are joined by arches of contrasting stone rectangles very similar to those on page 37 (top right). The simple repetition over such an enormous space makes me quite giddy. As if this weren't enough of a theatrical experience, suddenly you come upon a full Catholic church inside the mosque, its Gothic lines in such contrast to the voluptuous curves of the surrounding arches.

With their straight, easy-to-cut lines, rectangles are, of course, common in quilting. The wonderful Gee's Bend quilters, who come from the poorest part of America's South, use the rectangle in their freewheeling quilts with inspiring abandon—some stack up piles of brick shapes in strong colors to produce compositions that are as captivating as the very best contemporary paintings. The Gee's Bend quilters also often use the traditional log cabin motif, rectangles placed around a square of fabric, but, of course, take it to their own idiosyncratic extreme. I have also seen great log cabin oddities by other quilters and have an especially vivid recollection of an old log cabin design in a book on early American quilts in which the rectangles of the log cabin were placed in contrasting rows, creating bordered box shapes. Added to that, the scrappy rectangular bricks that made up the sashing on this quilt gave the whole composition a staccato excitement. Sashing is, obviously, a common place to incorporate rectangles on quilts old and new; I did just that for my Indigo Points on page 68, which made it so different from Clay Tiles on page 67, where the blocks butt up to each other without sashing.

Everywhere around us simple rectangles evoke varying visual moods. The graceful curve of bricks in an old English wall contrast so sharply with the modern tiles of a London highway underpass (opposite page, top). In its strong simplicity, my deep green and blue Tilt quilt holds its own against these brash tiles, which we found totally by chance. Making every other brick on the quilt a solid really underlines the simple geometry. Another strong use of rectangles, Belt and Braces (above) was inspired by a quilt from the 1800s. I put a lot more contrast into it than is usual in my patchwork, to really emphasize the geometric structure.

TILT

While leading a workshop in Germany, I viewed a collection of Asian textiles gathered by a world traveler with a great eye. The highlight for me was a religious wall hanging from Vietnam done in basic brick shapes in dark and medium shades of red. It was so simple yet I couldn't take my eyes off it. With memories of that piece in my mind's eye, I placed fabric rectangles on the design wall in Liza's studio in Pennsylvania, and in no time Tilt—in a palette inspired by Islamic pottery—was designed. A few weeks later, back in London, I spotted an underpass decorated with colorful, rectangular tiles laid out exactly like the fabric rectangles on Tilt. I knew right away we would photograph this quilt here.

See instructions on pages 46–49.

▲ BELT AND BRACES

It always thrills me to see a simple idea executed in such an exciting way that I can't take my eyes off it.
That was the case when an antique quilt collector showed me a bold nineteenth-century quilt. The powerful
grids of the original were done in checks and simple prints in dark tones against calico creams and pale
prints. When I decided to do my own version, I chose a contrasting autumnal palette. I think it has the feel
of a lumberjack shirt, so I call it Belt and Braces ("braces" is the British word for men's leather suspenders,
and wearing "belt and braces" is a common British expression that describes a cautious person).

See instructions on pages 50-52.

◄ TARGET LOG CABIN

Once again I take inspiration here from an antique, a log cabin done in a brown palette. Framing the sharply contrasting concentric squares of the log cabin blocks with brick borders creates a very graphic composition; the structure is so strong that it would read well even in a very low-contrast palette.

Although I'm content with this quilt overall, I do find the contrast between the very light prints and the darker ones a bit harsh. If I were to start again, I would choose fabrics with closer tones, to emulate the look of faded old quilts where the design emerges only after some close study, or even the look of the old stone setting where we did our photography, maybe all shades of grays and chalky pastels.

See instructions on pages 53–56.

STRIPESCAPE

I couldn't possibly sew all of the quilts I design and I am very grateful for the brilliant work of the sewers who work with me. But every now and then I try to stitch a quilt myself to experience the entire process. Stripescape was just such an experience. I cut long strips of striped fabrics in a range of rusts, pinks, and other rich medium-toned colors, being careful not to line up the stripes too carefully so there would be an organic unevenness to them. I sewed them in two blocks to create the quilt center. Then I sewed these two blocks together and added layers of strips across the two at the top and bottom. Each step of the way I stopped and pinned the work to my design wall so I could see how everything was jelling (something that isn't easy to do when someone else is sewing for me outside of my studio). I did the quilting by hand with running stitches, using warm, bright colors of cotton embroidery thread.

See instructions on pages 57–61.

TILT

This quilt is another good choice for a beginner. The wide border is composed of simple large rectangles, so once you have arranged the patches, the border is quick to finish. The nine blocks at the center will take a little longer to sew because each block consists of four triangles and a large rectangle—just enough of a challenge for a novice to keep the stitching interesting!

FINISHED SIZE
63" × 88" (160 cm × 223.5 cm)

MATERIALS
Use quilting cottons 44–45" (112–114 cm) wide

PATCHWORK FABRICS

Fabric A (center quilt "background" fabric): 3/4 yd (70 cm) of a solid-colored light-toned gray-green fabric—OR Kaffe Fassett *Shot Cotton* in Lichen

Fabric B (dark fabrics): 1/4–1/2 yd (25–46 cm) each of at least 10 different medium-toned and dark-toned medium-scale and large-scale prints in a rich luminous palette of blues, turquoises, violets, and purples, including a few with magenta accents; a total of approximately 4 yd (3.7 m)

Fabric C (light fabrics): 1/4–1/2 yd (25–46 cm) each of at least eight different light-toned fabrics (mostly in solid colors and a few monochromatic small-scale prints) in aquas and greens; a total of approximately 4 yd (3.7 m)

OTHER INGREDIENTS

Backing fabric: 5 yd (4.6 m) of desired fabric

Binding fabric: 3/4 yd (70 cm) extra of one of the fabric B prints

Cotton batting: 70" × 95" (175 cm × 240 cm)

Quilting thread: Medium green thread

Templates: Use templates GG, HH, JJ, and KK (see pages 184 and 185)

CUTTING PATCHES

Each of the nine blocks at the center of the quilt is made up of a large rectangle, two small triangles, and two large triangles. Cut the patches for these blocks first and the border patches last.

QUILT CENTER

9 short rectangles: Cut nine template-GG short rectangles from fabric B (darks), using at least seven different fabrics.

18 small triangles: Cut 18 template-HH triangles from fabric A (quilt center "background" fabric).

18 large triangles: Cut 18 template-JJ triangles from fabric A (quilt center "background" fabric).

BORDERS

180 long rectangles: Cut 90 template-KK long rectangles from fabric B (darks) and 90 from fabric C (lights)—for a total of 180 long rectangles. (To link the border and quilt center as we did on our version of this quilt, you can cut four of the 90 light-toned rectangles from fabric A.)

MAKING BLOCKS

Make the blocks using the seam allowance marked on the templates.

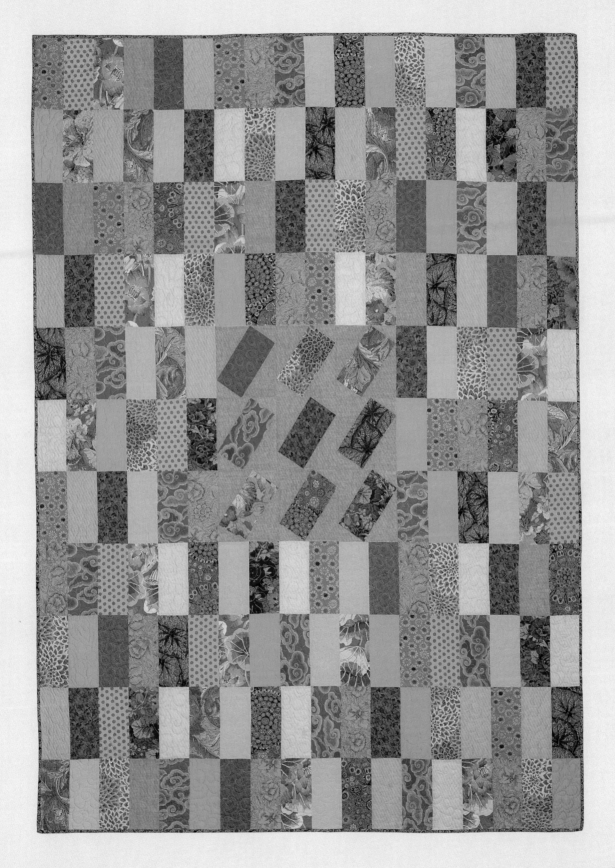

A corner of Tilt in front of the tiles that are so like the quilt's layout and proportions. The saturated, luminous blues work amazingly well against the blast of bright contrasting tiles. You could do this quilt in any favored color range. Or what about a very gypsy approach to look like the buddha robe on page 36?

9 center-quilt blocks: For each of the nine center-quilt blocks, sew two template-HH triangles, and two template-JJ triangles to a template-GG short rectangle as shown in the block diagram.

Tilt Block

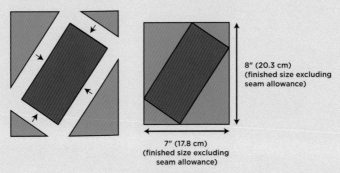

8″ (20.3 cm)
(finished size excluding
seam allowance)

7″ (17.8 cm)
(finished size excluding
seam allowance)

ASSEMBLING TOP

Arrange the blocks as shown on the assembly diagram (page 49), either laying them out on the floor or sticking them to a cotton-flannel design wall. For the quilt center, position three rows of three blocks. Surround the center with three horizontal rows of six rectangles at each side and four horizontal rows of 18 rectangles at the top and bottom, alternating the dark (fabric B) and light (fabric C) rectangles.

Using the seam allowance marked on the templates throughout, first sew the blocks for the quilt center together in three horizontal rows of three blocks, then sew the three rows together as shown on the assembly diagram.

For each side border, sew the rectangles together in horizontal rows, then sew the rows together. Sew together the rectangles for the top and bottom borders in the same way. Sew the side borders to the quilt center first, then sew on the top and bottom borders.

FINISHING QUILT

Press the quilt top. Layer the quilt top, batting, and backing, then baste the layers together (see page 181).

Using medium green thread, machine-quilt meandering leaf shapes over the quilt.

Trim the quilt edges. Then cut the binding fabric on the bias and sew it on around the edge of the quilt (see page 181).

Tilt Assembly

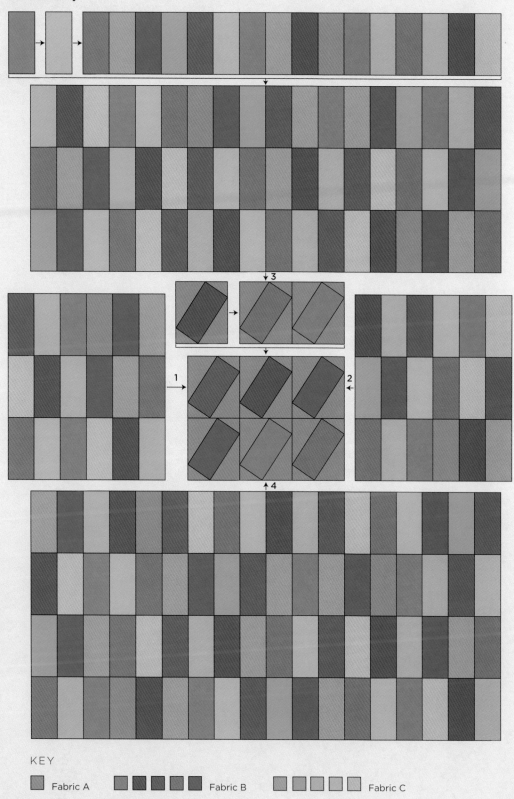

KEY

◼ Fabric A ◼◼◼◼◼ Fabric B ◼◼◼◼◼ Fabric C

BELT AND BRACES

Despite appearances, there are no difficult seams at all on this masculine-looking quilt. The rectangles, squares, and triangles are sewn together in simple strips and sections. All you have to do is follow the block diagram carefully and stitch the pieces together in the correct order. Then take your time arranging the finished blocks into a well-balanced whole.

FINISHED SIZE

64 1/2" × 75 3/4" (164 cm × 192.5 cm)

MATERIALS

Use quilting cottons 44–45" (112–114 cm) wide

PATCHWORK FABRICS

Fabric A (lights): 1/4 yd (25 cm) each of at least 10 light-toned small-scale prints, dots, and checks in pinks, grays, mint, and mustard yellow; a total of 2 1/2 yd (2.3 m)

Fabric B (darks): 1/4–1/2 yd (25–46 cm) each of at least 13 different medium-toned and dark-toned small-scale prints and checks in a husky masculine palette of cobalt blue, ocher, rusts, pinks, and burgundys; a total of 3 3/4 yd (3.5 m)

Fabric C (border fabric): 2 yd (1.9 m) of a medium-scale organic print in navy, rust, gold, apple green, and bean brown

OTHER INGREDIENTS

Backing fabric: 4 yd (3.7 m) of desired fabric

Binding fabric: 3/4 yd (70 cm) of a medium-scale monochromatic print in burgundy

Cotton batting: 72" × 83" (180 cm × 210 cm)

Quilting thread: Medium taupe thread

Templates: Use template X (see page 185), and templates E, F, and G (see page 191)

CUTTING PATCHES

30 blocks: For the first block, choose a single fabric A (one of the lights) and a single fabric B (one of the darks). From the light fabric, cut four template-X squares and eight template-G triangles; and from the dark fabric, cut six template-X squares, five template-E rectangles, four template-G triangles, and four template-F corner triangles. Cut patches for each of the remaining 29 blocks in the same way, using a different color scheme for each block.

4 border strips: From fabric C, cut two strips 4 1/2" × 68 1/4" (11.4 cm × 173.4 cm) for the side borders; then cut two strips 4 1/2" × 65" (11.4 cm × 165.1 cm) for the top and bottom borders.

MAKING BLOCKS

Make the blocks using the seam allowance marked on the templates.

30 blocks: Using the light and dark patches cut for each block, first arrange the block and then sew it together as shown in the block diagram.

Belt and Braces Block

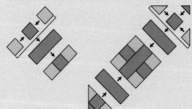

11 5/16" (28.7 cm) square (finished size excluding seam allowance)

ASSEMBLING TOP

Arrange the quilt center as shown on the assembly diagram (page 52), either laying out the patches on the floor or sticking them to a cotton-flannel design wall. Arrange the quilt in six horizontal rows of five blocks each.

Islamic tiles from the Alhambra in Spain have inspired me for years (above top). The little stars at the corners of rectangle sashing are such a delicate statement, and the monochrome frames make the rich tones of the glazed tiles really sing. I did a cotton knit design from this that worked a treat in dark tones with deep ocher sashing. The fresh blue and white grid (above) is set off nicely by the shadow on each section of the lattice, but I prefer my Belt and Braces version of the simple lattice, which infuses it with sumptuous color and movement.

KEY

Fabric A

Fabric B

Fabric C

Using the seam allowance marked on the templates throughout, sew the blocks together in horizontal rows, then sew the rows together. Sew the long side borders to the quilt center, then sew on the top and bottom borders.

FINISHING QUILT

Press the quilt top. Layer the quilt top, batting, and backing, then baste the layers together (see page 181).

Using medium taupe thread, machine-quilt the entire quilt with meandering curving shapes, such as stylized leaves.

Trim the quilt edges. Then cut the binding fabric on the bias and sew it on around the edge of the quilt (see page 181).

Belts and Braces Assembly

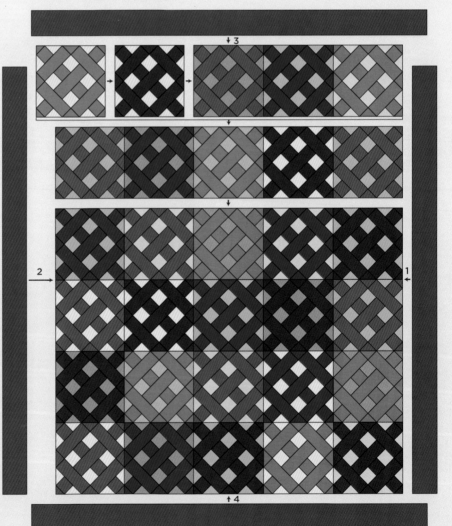

TARGET LOG CABIN

The traditional log cabin technique is used to make the big blocks on this quilt—each block starts with a center square to which narrow rectangular patches (called logs) are added in rings. Notice how the grayed-down tones of the Kaffe Fassett and Philip Jacobs Rowan fabrics chosen for this quilt allow the red pinwheels and red log cabin centers to really stand out.

FINISHED SIZE
93" × 93" (236 cm × 236 cm)

MATERIALS
Use quilting cottons 44–45" (112–114 cm) wide

PATCHWORK FABRICS

Fabric A (log cabin center squares and light pinwheel triangles): 1/2 yd (46 cm) each of a medium-toned solid in lacquer-red and a medium-toned polka dot in lacquer-red—OR 1/2 yd (46 cm) each of the following two Rowan fabrics:

Shot Cotton in Persimmon and *Spot* in Tomato

Fabric B (lights for strip patches): 1/4–1/2 yd (25–46 cm) each of at least 14 different light-toned small-scale prints (and a polka dot) in pinks, lavender blues, oranges, silver gray, taupe, and ochers—OR 1/4–1/2 yd (25–46 cm) each of the following 14 Rowan fabrics:

Paper Fans in Vintage, Ochre, and Yellow; *Persimmons* in Orange, Pink, and Opal; *Star Flowers* in Taupe; *Aboriginal Dot* in Rose and Blue; *Lichen* in Pink; *Asian Circles* in Ochre; *Spot* in Grey; *Dahlia Blooms* in Pink; and *Millefiore* in Orange

Fabric C (darks for strip patches): 1/4–1/2 yd (25–46 cm) each of at least 13 different dark-medium-toned and dark-toned small-scale prints in browns, maroons, turquoise, cobalt blues, purple, and bottle green—OR 1/4–1/2 yd (25–46 cm) each of the following 13 Rowan fabrics:

Millefiore in Red; *Winding Floral* in Indigo; *Paperweight* in Gypsy and Teal; *Begonia Leaf* in Maroon; *Roman Glass* in Jewel; *Dancing Leaves* in Moss; *Spot* in Burgundy; *Big Blooms* in Rust and Teal; *Star Flowers* in Prune; *Paisley Jungle* in Moss; and *Lichen* in Brown

Fabric D (dark pinwheel triangles): 1/2 yd (46 cm) of a dark-toned small-scale moss-green print—OR Rowan *Stencil Carnation* in Sludge

OTHER INGREDIENTS

Backing fabric: 9 yd (8.3 m) of desired fabric

Binding fabric: 1 yd (92 cm) of a monochromatic small-scale print in rust

Cotton batting: 100" × 100" (250 cm × 250 cm)

Quilting thread: Medium taupe thread

Templates: Use templates R, S, T, U, V, W, X, Y, and Z (see page 185)

CUTTING PATCHES

The center squares for each of the 36 log cabin blocks are cut from one of the two red fabrics (fabric A). The strip patches that form the alternating light and dark rings (logs) around the center square are cut from fabric B (lights) and fabric C (darks). Half of the log cabin blocks end with a light ring of fabric and half with a dark ring of fabric, so cut patches for "light-edged" and "dark-edged" blocks as explained here.

18 light-edged log cabin blocks: For the first block, cut a template-X center square from fabric A. Then from a single fabric B (a light fabric), cut two patches each with templates R, S, T, U, V, and W. Lastly, from a single fabric C (a dark fabric), cut two patches each with templates S, T, U, and V. Cut the patches for the remaining 17 light-edged log cabin blocks in the same way.

18 dark-edged log cabin blocks: For the first block, cut a template-X center square from fabric A. Then from a single fabric C (a dark fabric), cut two patches each with templates R, S, T, U, V, and W. Lastly, from a single fabric B (a light fabric), cut two patches each with templates S, T, U, and V. Cut the patches for the remaining 17 dark-edged log cabin blocks in the same way.

Log Cabin Templates

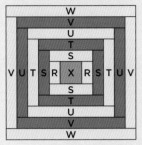

Use the templates marked on this diagram for the center square and the strip patches.

Log Cabin Block Assembly

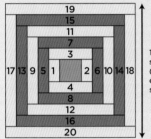

12" (30.5 cm) square (finished size excluding seam allowance)

Starting at the center, sew on the strip patches in this order.

Pinwheel Block

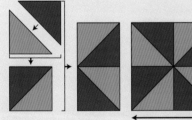

3" (7.6 cm) square (finished size excluding seam allowance)

49 small pinwheel blocks: For each of the 49 pinwheel blocks, cut four matching template-Y triangles from a fabric A and four matching template-Y triangles from fabric D—for a total of 196 triangles in fabric A and 196 triangles in fabric D.

84 sashing rectangles: For each of the 84 sashing rectangles, cut six template-Z patches from an assortment of fabric B (lights) and six from an assortment of fabric C (darks)—for a total of 504 light patches and 504 dark patches.

MAKING BLOCKS

Make the blocks using the seam allowance marked on the templates.

36 log cabin blocks: Using the 20 strip patches and the center square cut for each block, arrange each block as shown in the Log Cabin Templates diagram. Then sew each block together as shown in the Log Cabin Block Assembly diagram, starting by sewing the two template-R strips to opposite sides of the center square and adding the remaining patches in the order given.

49 small pinwheel blocks: Using the four matching template-Y triangles cut from fabric A and the four template-Y triangles cut from fabric D for each block, make the blocks as shown in the block diagram.

84 sashing rectangles: Using the 12 template-Z patches (six light and six dark) for each sashing rectangle, arrange each rectangle with alternating light and dark patches to form a strip 3 1/2" (8.9 cm) by 12 1/2" (31.8 cm). Sew the 12 patches of each rectangle together to make 84 sashing rectangles.

ASSEMBLING TOP

Arrange the quilt center as shown on the assembly diagram (page 56), either laying out the patches on the floor or sticking them to a design wall. Arrange the log cabin blocks in six horizontal rows of six blocks with sashing rectangles (and pinwheel blocks) in between them. Keeping a nice balance of color, position the light-edged and dark-edged log cabin blocks at random.

Using the seam allowance marked on the templates throughout, sew the seven horizontal rows of sashing rectangles and pinwheel blocks together, then sew together the six horizontal rows of log cabin blocks and sashing rectangles. Sew the rows together.

FINISHING QUILT

Press the quilt top. Layer the quilt top, batting, and backing, then baste the layers together (see page 181).

Using medium taupe thread, machine-quilt a gently curving line along the center of each ring (log) in the log cabin blocks and through the center of each sashing patch. Then machine-quilt a freeform shape in the center square of each block. Lastly, stitch-in-the-ditch around all patches in the pinwheel blocks.

Trim the quilt edges. Then cut the binding fabric on the bias and sew it on around the edge of the quilt (see page 181).

Target Log Cabin Assembly

KEY

Fabric A   Fabric B   Fabric C   Fabric D

STRIPESCAPE

Use any Kaffe Fassett stripe fabrics for your very own interpretation of this easy-to-make quilt, or use up the stripe scraps in your collection. All the stripe fabrics are cut into two different widths and then, as the quilt is arranged on the floor or design wall, the patches are cut into random lengths from these striped strips. It couldn't be easier or more fun!

FINISHED SIZE

66" × 70 1/2" (168 cm × 184 cm)

MATERIALS

Use quilting cottons 44–45" (112–114 cm) wide

PATCHWORK FABRICS

1/4–1 yd (25–92 cm) of at least 15 different medium-toned and dark-toned narrow and broad woven stripes in mostly rusts, ocher, reds, lavenders, and pinks, with accents in shades of turquoise and dark moss-green; a total of approximately 11–13 yd (10–12 m)

OTHER INGREDIENTS

Backing fabric: 4 1/4 yd (4 m) of desired fabric

Binding fabric: 3/4 yd (70 cm) extra of one of the stripe fabrics

Cotton batting: 73" × 77" (185 cm × 200 cm)

Quilting thread: Dusky rose and rust stranded cotton embroidery floss (or an embroidery thread as thick as three strands of floss) for hand quilting

PREPARING FABRIC STRIPS

All the short strips that make up this quilt are cut either 2" (5.5 cm) or 3" (8 cm) wide, with the exception of the strips for one pieced strip in the center right panel that are cut 1 1/2" (4 cm) wide and a large patch 5 1/2" (14.5 cm) wide in the same panel. Because you will be designing the quilt panels on your design wall as you cut the strips to random lengths, it is easiest to precut some long lengths of strips before you begin the first panel (the center left panel). Follow the stripes when cutting most of the strips; for a little extra variety in the mixture, you can cut a few with the stripes running slightly askew.

Narrow strips: Cut some long strips 2" (5.5 cm) wide from each of the different stripe fabrics, with the stripes running parallel to the long side of each strip.

Wide strips: Cut some long strips 3" (8 cm) wide from each of the different stripe fabrics, with the stripes running parallel to the long side of each strip. Most of the strips used on the quilt are 3" (8 cm) wide, so you will use about three times as many of these wide strips.

CUTTING AND ARRANGING PATCHES

Arrange the strip patches as you cut them (see the assembly diagram on page 61), either laying them out on the floor or sticking them to a design wall. Begin with the center left panel, followed by the center right panel, and lastly the top and bottom panels. Cut more long strips when you need them.

CENTER LEFT PANEL

The center left panel of the quilt is made up of 19 horizontal rows of strip patches. Cut two to five strip patches of random lengths from different fabrics for each horizontal row, making sure that patches cut from the same fabric do not touch each other. Arrange the strip patches for each row end to end, and make sure that when placed end to end (and just touching) they measure at least 42 1/2" (110 cm) across the horizontal row—this allows for seam allowances and for trimming the pieced strips to 39" (99.5 cm) during the assembly process.

Here are some of the rectangles that inspired Stripescape. Old scrap wood used on shacks and doors get me every time—how luminous this range of greens, blues, and wood tones is. And the rectangular shape of boxcars in large port cities can set me off on dozens of designs. Even the neutral world of this sandstone wall serves up a delightful array of shapes and tones for inspiration.

Starting at the top of the panel, cut and arrange the patches in 19 rows of wide and narrow strip patches of random lengths as follows:

Three horizontal rows of wide strip patches; one row of narrow strip patches; three rows of wide strip patches; one row of narrow strip patches; two rows of wide strip patches; one row of narrow strip patches (for added interest, sew together several very short strip patches and add this in as one of the strip patches in this row); one row of wide strip patches; one row of narrow strip patches; two rows of wide strip patches; one row of narrow strip patches; and three rows of wide strip patches.

CENTER RIGHT PANEL

The center right panel of the quilt is made up of 20 horizontal rows of strip patches. Cut two to four strip patches of random lengths from different fabrics for each horizontal row, making sure that patches cut from the same fabric do not touch each other and paying attention to how the patches look along the left side in relation to the center left panel. Arrange the strip patches for each row end to end, and make sure that when placed end to end (and just touching) they measure at least 31 1/2" (82 cm) across the horizontal row—this allows for seam allowances and for trimming the pieced strips to 28" (71.5 cm) during the assembly process.

Starting at the top of the panel, cut and arrange the patches in 20 rows of wide and narrow strip patches of random lengths as follows:

One row of narrow strip patches; three rows of wide strip patches; one row of narrow strip patches; one row of wide strip patches; one row of narrow strip patches; two rows of wide strip patches—for added interest, cut a large patch 5 1/2" (14.5 cm) wide and of random length to position at one end of these two rows (see assembly diagram); four more rows of wide strip patches; two rows of narrow strip patches (you can use a single strip patch for the second of these rows); two rows of wide strip patches; one row of narrow strip patches; one row of wide strip patches; and for the last row of strip patches, use very narrow strips cut 1 1/2" (4 cm) wide.

TOP PANEL

The top panel of the quilt is made up of six horizontal rows of strip patches. Cut four to five strip patches of random lengths from different fabrics for each horizontal row, paying attention to how the patches look along the lower edge in relation to the center right and left panels. Arrange the strip patches for each row end to end, and make sure that when placed end to end (and just touching) they measure at least 70" (180 cm) across the horizontal row—this allows for seam allowances and for trimming the pieced strips to 66 1/2" (169.5 cm) during the assembly process.

Starting at the top of the panel, cut and arrange the patches in six rows of wide and narrow strip patches of random lengths as follows:

Three rows of wide strip patches; one row of narrow strip patches; one row of wide strip patches; and one row of narrow strip patches.

Many people avoid stripes because they feel they must line them up carefully. I deliberately sewed many of them slightly off-grain in this quilt to capture a more random and wavelike look. Then I hand-quilted the patchwork with long running stitches in glowing colors.

BOTTOM PANEL

The bottom panel of the quilt is made up of six horizontal rows of strip patches. Cut four to six strip patches of random lengths from different fabrics for each horizontal row, paying attention to how the patches look along the top edge in relation to the center right and left panels. Arrange the strip patches for each row end to end, and make sure that when placed end to end (and just touching) they measure at least 70" (180 cm) across the horizontal row—this allows for seam allowances and for trimming the pieced strips to 66 1/2" (169.5 cm) during the assembly process.

Starting at the top of the panel, cut and arrange the patches in six rows of wide strip patches of random lengths.

ASSEMBLING TOP

Make any last-minute adjustments to the color and stripe arrangement of the four panels.

CENTER LEFT PANEL

Using a 1/4" (7.5 mm) seam allowance throughout, sew together the patches in each of the 19 horizontal rows. Then press the seams open, and trim each pieced strip to 39" (99.5 cm) long. Sew together the pieced strips, alternating the stitching direction on each long seam to prevent distortion.

CENTER RIGHT PANEL

Sew this panel together as for the center left panel, but trim each pieced strip to 28" (71.5 cm) long before sewing the strips together.

TOP AND BOTTOM PANELS

Sew each of these panels together as for the center left panel, but trim each pieced strip to 66 1/2" (169.5 cm) long before sewing the strips together.

JOINING PANELS

Sew the center left panel to the center right panel. Then sew the top and bottom panels to the quilt center.

FINISHING QUILT

Press the quilt top. Layer the quilt top, batting, and backing, then baste the layers together (see page 181).

Using three strands of cotton embroidery floss in dusky rose or rust, hand-quilt horizontal lines of short running stitches across the width of the quilt. Position the lines of stitches 1/2–1" (12 mm–2.5 cm) apart. The hand-stitched quilting doesn't have to be absolutely straight—a little wiggle is okay.

Trim the quilt edges. Then cut the binding fabric on the bias and sew it on around the edge of the quilt (see page 181).

Stripescape Assembly

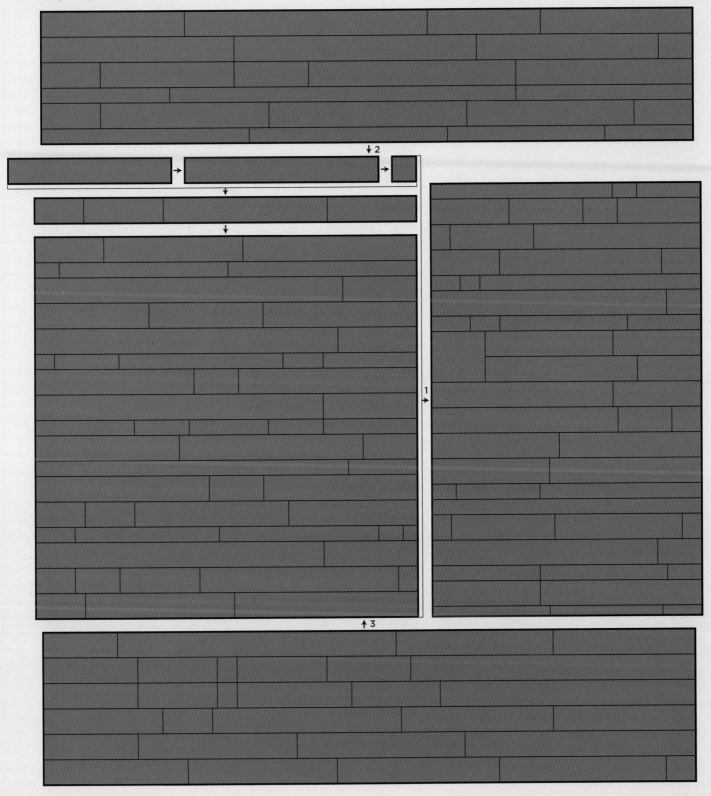

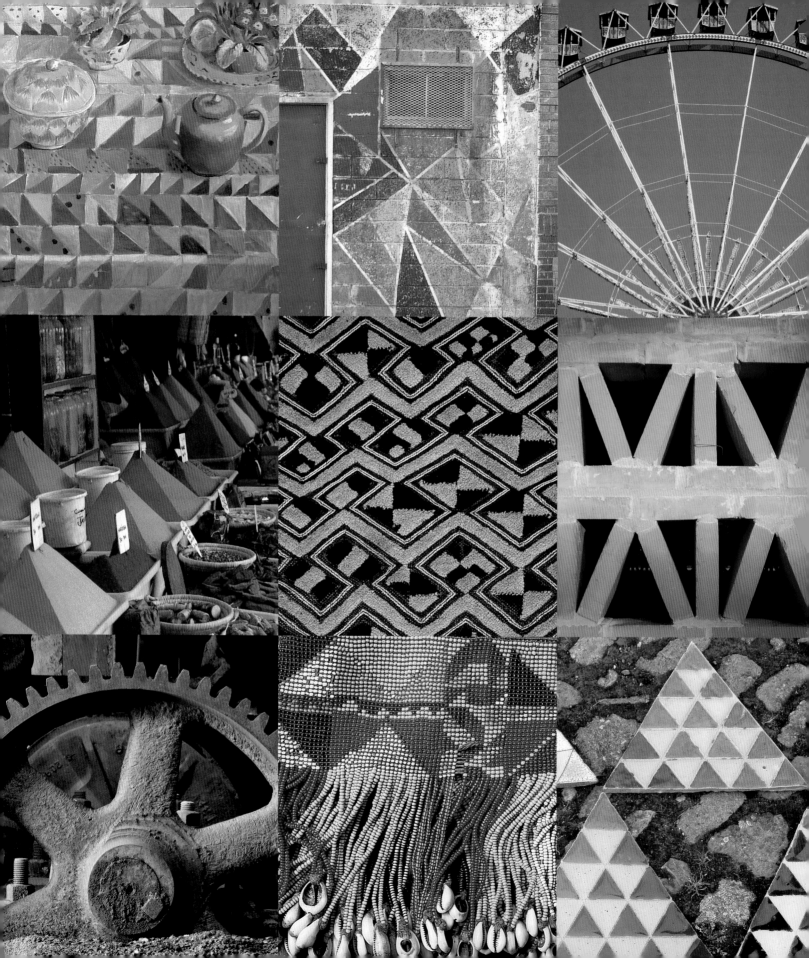

TRIANGLES

Open your eyes and you will spot triangles everywhere. I have seen wonderful examples on decorated columns from ancient Rome, on Kuba textiles from Africa, and on Native American woven baskets. I have even spotted chocolates and cookies in this three-cornered shape. In a market in the Moroccan town of Essaouira, gold, amber, and deep brown pyramids of spices—perfect three-dimensional triangles—had me running to my hotel for my camera (see left).

Islamic art is another great source of triangles, especially Islamic tiles, which are often made in triangular and diamond shapes and then combined on the walls of mosques in gorgeous star designs. In the 1970s Sherlee Lantz published a needlepoint book called *Trianglepoint* that featured nothing but designs inspired by triangles. Her sources were Persian miniatures, Ottoman tiles, and Iranian brickwork. Any book on ethnic textiles, such as John Gillow's and Bryan Sentance's *World Textiles*, will show you at a glance how many cultures use the triangle in lace, embroidery, weaving, beading, and dyeing. Sometimes I find myself studying intricate designs for ages before I realize that they are exhibiting yet another clever use of triangles. But the best examples of triangles I've ever seen is the tile floor at Winchester Cathedral that inspired Clay Tiles (page 67)—simple repetitions of contrasting triangles in rows, each tile glazed to a different variation of tone.

In the industrial world, great iron bridges and giraffe-like cranes are often reinforced with triangular shapes. Because they take such a battering they are often distressed to an intriguing patina. The bridge on the first page of this book is a good example—the rich incrustation of rust and old paint makes a gorgeous smolder of a backdrop for Clay Tiles. Also, heavy tram and tractor wheels have bold structures that create negative triangles.

The Art Deco era of design is filled with triangular details. Probably for Americans the most iconic is the Chrysler Building, which adds an elegant note to the New York City skyline. It is crowned with gorgeous crescents of triangles whose strong profile reads for miles around (see page 63).

Triangles often make a starring appearance in my knitting (see page 63, bottom center and right). They are a no-brainer to knit and their sharp profiles add such jaunty spice to a design. I'm sure that's why you find triangles so often in African beading and Kuba cloth; they flow so naturally to anyone improvising with textile shapes, and to such good effect. Just think of the lines of triangular flags to celebrate parties, hung on boats, or to catch attention at car sale lots. When I was in Cambodia I came across a primitive village temple, the ceiling of which was covered in scrappy triangles in bright colors. It gave me a shiver of delight that such spare means could create such a joyous effect.

In the quilting world, when you slice a square from corner to corner, you create the wildly useful triangle. Then the real fun begins. Placing two triangles together in contrasting tones has been the cornerstone of thousands of quilts throughout history. Traditional quilt designs like the bear's claw, lady of the lake, flying geese, pinwheel, and hourglass all rely on triangles and have been fascinating quilters for centuries, but even simple rows of triangles are eye-catching, as you can see in Clay Tiles (page 67) and Indigo Points (page 68).

Displays like these pyramids of deep autumn-toned spices in a Moroccan market give me endless inspiration (opposite page, top). Markets with piled-up fruits and vegetables, stacks of cloth or cans, even plastic buckets on display can spark many a happy idea for textile designers. My still life (above) painted in the 1980s shows the old silk quilt that led to my best knitting design of that time, called Super Triangles. Those triangles turned in different directions have a very lively profile. Even when they are lined up symmetrically they are very rhythmic, as on Clay Tiles (opposite page, bottom).

◄ HAZE KILIM

When Liza first proposed doing a quilt book together nearly ten years ago, she told me that she thought the Carpet Coat from my first book, Glorious Knits, would be perfectly gorgeous as a quilt. But it took me all these years to successfully interpret her idea.

Haze Kilim is made entirely of triangles. The intensely striated effect is created by cutting the patches from string-pieced fabrics (fabrics made from thin strips sewn together). We used my striped fabrics woven in India in the duskiest colors so the stripes would merge together.

I was excited to find this mossy stone wall and gate to shoot the quilt on. The dark London setting really makes the colors glow. Imagine how delicate this quilt could be in alabaster tones, grays, soft ochers, creams, and whites with dashes of lavenders, sky blues, and mint greens.

See instructions on pages 70–74.

► CLAY TILES

When I saw a photo of some triangular floor tiles at Winchester Cathedral, I knew I would design a quilt around them. It was the earthy tones of the glazes that had me salivating. To capture that feeling, I chose organic prints, mostly from Carla Miller.

I so often use brilliant high color or soft pastels that it was a relief to explore this muted earthy palette—it reminds me of old stamps and the endpapers of books. I like the way the gray, blues, and lavenders gently lift the ocher and brown mood. Any collection of textural earth-tone prints will work here. This concept would also be perfect in a neutral palette, such as soft grays and grayed-down pastels with pale creams and whites. I think this decaying London bridge was a good setting to harmonize with the corroded metal look of the prints I used.

See instructions on pages 75–77.

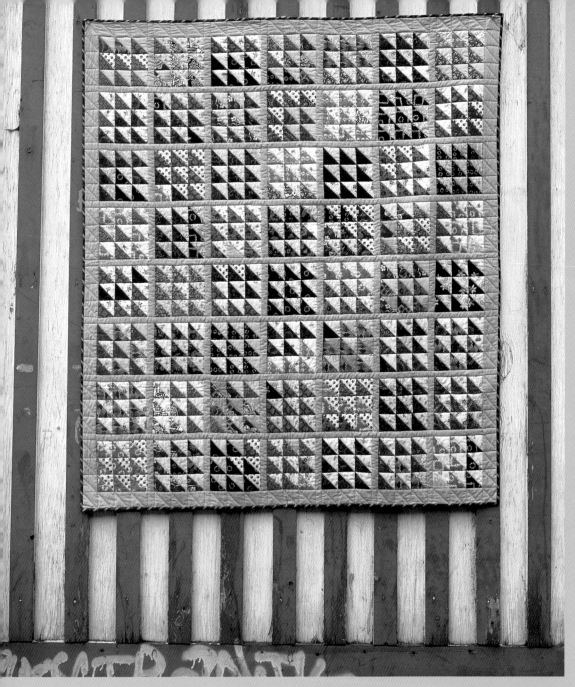

◄ INDIGO POINTS

This is another spinoff of that clay tile floor at Winchester Cathedral. This time I made my quilt in a collection of indigo prints Liza had been saving. Blue and white is such a classic color combination. When I think of Dutch tiles, Japanese and Chinese porcelains, and African tie-dye batiks, I am struck again and again by how deeply beautiful it can be, yet, on the other hand, it can be deadly boring in pedestrian hands. To keep this quilt lively, I added a lot of variation in my blue prints and my paler background "whites." The odd stab of lavender, even pink, gives the scene energy. The gray sashing does stop the interplay of points from block to block; leave it out if you prefer the way Clay Tiles (page 67) looks.

I love this old wooden fence. Painted dusty blue and white, it works well with the fresher blue and white of the quilt.

See instructions on pages 78–81.

► EARTHY MITERED BOXES

I am always excited and curious to see how an idea is transformed by a total change of color mood. For example, for my book Passionate Patchwork, I made a quilt called Mitered Boxes with classic blue-and-white shirt striping materials. It had very clean, professional-looking squares made out of triangles. Later, after I had a large range of warm-toned striped fabrics woven in India, it seemed a good idea to revisit this quilt, and that is what you see here. The deep earthy tones make it so different from the fresh original (and are so nicely shown off on the weathered wall of this Victorian monument).

For a third version of this great layout, how about using the joyous palette of Striped Donut (page 16)? Using those sorts of stripes in warm pastels would look gorgeous, if slightly less masculine than all the browns I used.

See instructions on pages 82–85.

HAZE KILIM

This quilt is made using a patchwork technique called strip or string piecing. Before any of the patches are cut, the patchwork fabrics are all cut into thin strips, sorted into lights and darks, and sewn (or pieced) back together in a random sequence to create sheets of unique light and dark fabrics. Any fabrics can be used with this technique, but stripes intensify the effect.

FINISHED SIZE
72 1/4" × 72 1/4" (183.5 cm × 183.5 cm)

MATERIALS
Use quilting cottons 44–45" (112–114 cm) wide

PATCHWORK FABRICS

Fabric A (darks): 1/2 yd (46 cm) each of at least 10 different dark-toned multicolored woven stripes and ikat or washy batik stripes in blues, purples, reds, and green-browns; a total of approximately 5 yd (4.6 m)

Fabric B (lights): 1/2 yd (46 cm) each of at least 10 different light-toned multicolored woven stripes and ikat or washy batik stripes in oranges, moss greens, soft blues, and light terra-cottas; a total of approximately 5 yd (4.6 m)

OTHER INGREDIENTS

Backing fabric: 4 1/2 yd (4.1 m) of desired fabric

Binding fabric: 3/4 yd (70 cm) of a stripe

Cotton batting: 79" (200 cm) square

Quilting thread: Medium taupe thread

Templates: Use templates F, G, H, and J (see pages 186 and 187)

SPECIAL FABRIC NOTE

If desired, you can make this quilt using Kaffe Fassett fabrics. All 22 of Kaffe Fassett *Haze Stripes* and all six of Kaffe Fassett *Ikat Feathers* were used for the quilt shown here.

PREPARING STRING-PIECED FABRICS

All the patches for the quilt top are cut from string-pieced fabrics. Preparing the fabrics takes time, and you will get the best results if you don't rush.

CUTTING AND SORTING

Cut all the fabrics into narrow strips with the stripes on the fabrics running parallel to the long side of each strip. Cut the strips in random widths 1–3 1/4" (2.5–8.5 cm) wide.

Sort the dark strips (fabric A strips) into four groups of similar colors—blues, purples, reds, and green-browns. Each group will be sewn together to make a new "fabric," so take your time in selecting the strips for each group. Some colors can be used in two groups, but keep the overall look of the four groups predominantly blues, purples, reds, or green-browns.

Next sort the light strips (fabric B strips) into four groups of similar colors—oranges, moss greens, soft blues, and light terra-cottas. Sort them in the same way as for the dark strips, keeping the overall look of the fours groups predominantly oranges, moss greens, soft blues, and light terra-cottas, but overlapping some colors in two groups.

PIECING STRIPS

Lay out each of the eight groups of strips in a random arrangement, aligning the strips side by side. Using a 1/4" (6 mm) seam allowance and stitching along the long edges of the strips, sew together the strips in each group to make four separate fabric-A sheets of pieced strips and four separate fabric-B sheets of pieced strips.

PRESSING AND STARCHING

Press all the seams open on each of the eight sheets of pieced strips. Then starch the sheets with a strong starch to make the fabric as stiff as possible and press again. Almost all the seams on this quilt are sewn along bias edges, so it

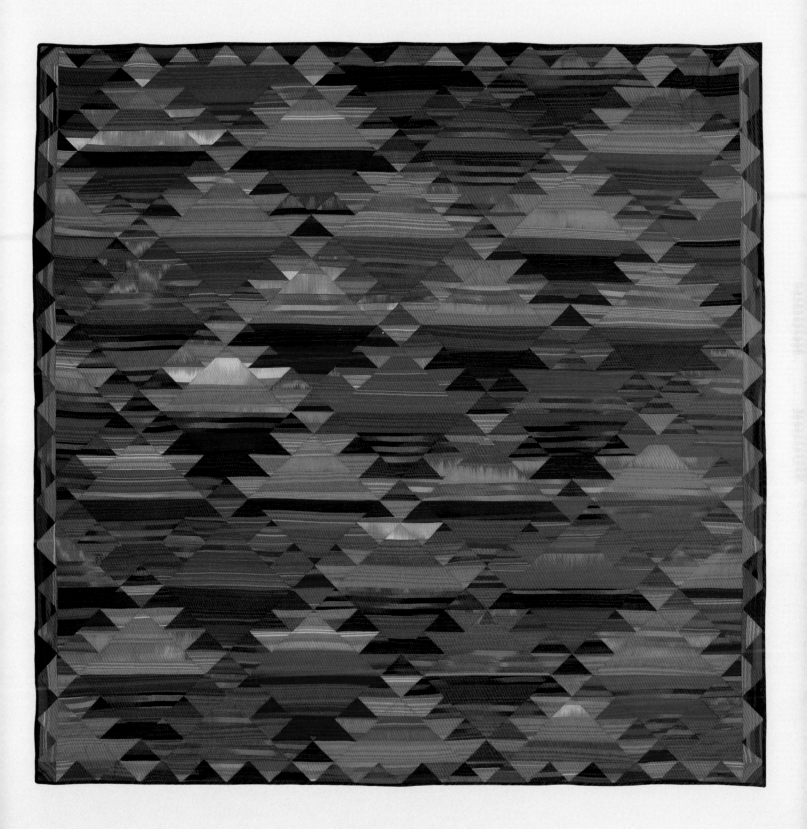

When I first started knitting I looked everywhere for motifs with which to experiment and was often inspired by old quilt blocks. Such was the case when I was knitting the design shown here. The format is similar to that of Haze Kilim, but the lights and darks are arranged in a different way, which alters the effect.

is important to use a strong starch and to make an effort to keep the pieced fabrics and the cut pieces flat until the top border has been sewn on.

CUTTING PATCHES

The desired effect for the quilt center is for each toothed shape to look as if it were cut from a single fabric, so when cutting the sets of "matching" triangles for a toothed shape, cut from the same area of a pieced fabric sheet. You can cut randomly from the fabric-A and fabric-B sheets, as there is no need to cut an equal number of toothed shapes from each fabric sheet. Remember to align the stripes with the grain-line marker (the arrow) on the template so that all the stripes will run across the width of the quilt.

Once the matching sets of triangles for each of the toothed shapes have been cut, make sure you carefully keep them together (and flat).

QUILT CENTER

28 dark-toned toothed triangles: Cut one large template-F triangle from fabric A; then cut seven small template-H triangles from the same sheet of fabric A for the teeth around the large triangle.

Cut 27 more large template-F triangles from fabric A and for each of these cut seven roughly matching small template-H triangles—for a total of 28 roughly matching sets.

28 light-toned toothed triangles: Following the instructions for the dark-toned toothed shapes, cut a total of 28 roughly matching sets (of one large triangle and seven small triangles) from fabric B.

8 dark-toned toothed half-triangles: The side edges of the quilt need to be filled in with toothed half-triangles. Note that the reverse templates are needed for some of the shapes so that the stripes are running in the correct direction.

Cut one medium-sized template-G triangle from fabric A; then cut three small template-H triangles and one small template-J triangle from the same sheet of fabric A for the teeth around the half-triangle. Cut three more medium-size template-G triangles from fabric A; and for each of these, cut three full teeth (template H) and one half-tooth (template J)—for a total of four roughly matching sets.

For the toothed half-triangles on the other side edge of the quilt, cut four more rough matching sets, but for these use templates G reverse, H, and J reverse.

8 light-toned toothed half-triangles: Cut a total of eight roughly matching sets in the same way as for the dark-toned toothed half-triangles, but from fabric B.

BORDER

64 dark-toned triangles: Cut 64 template-H triangles from various sheets of fabric A.

60 light-toned triangles: Cut 60 template-H triangles from various sheets of fabric B.

Haze Kilim Assembly

KEY

■ Fabric A   ■ Fabric B

The Haze Kilim quilt was inspired by a knit pattern that in turn was inspired by a kilim carpet I found in London. I like to find bold patterns to back my quilts, as you can see here. This backing is Lotus Leaf, one of my most popular prints.

8 light-toned half-triangles: Cut four template-J triangles from various sheets of fabric B. Then cut four template-J-reverse triangles—for a total of 8 light-toned triangles.

4 corner squares: For the corner squares on the border, cut four template-J triangles from fabric A and four from fabric B, but *ignore the grain line* on the template and align the stripes on each of the eight triangles with the longest edge of the template.

ASSEMBLING TOP

It is essential to arrange the quilt center as shown on the assembly diagram (page 73) before sewing, either laying out the patches on the floor or sticking them to a cotton-flannel design wall. Carefully keeping the matching sets together, alternate the light and dark groups of toothed triangles.

Using the seam allowance marked on the templates throughout, sew the patches together in eight horizontal rows as shown on the assembly diagram. Then sew the eight horizontal rows together.

For each of the two side borders, sew together 16 dark triangles and 15 light triangles as shown; then, sew a light template-J triangle to one end and a light template-J-reverse triangle to the other end.

For the top and bottom borders, sew together 16 dark triangles, 15 light triangles, and two light half-triangles as for the side borders.

For each of the four corner squares, sew together one of the dark and one of the light triangles cut for the corners. Sew one pieced corner square to each end of the top and bottom borders.

Sew the side borders to the center quilt, then sew on the top and bottom borders.

FINISHING QUILT

Press the quilt top. Layer the quilt top, batting, and backing, then baste the layers together (see page 181).

Using medium taupe thread, stitch-in-the-ditch around each patch. Then machine-quilt back and forth in a continuous line inside each patch so these quilting lines follow the direction of the stripes (turn the stitching at each end with a curve).

Trim the quilt edges. Then cut the binding fabric on the bias and sew it on around the edge of the quilt (see page 181).

CLAY TILES

For those who want to break away from square patches for the first time, this triangles format couldn't be easier to stitch. You can have all the fun of playing with color placement with only the most basic sewing effort. Use up fabric scraps or purchase a unique new palette. For an effect similar to this version, choose antiqued hues and avoid very light-toned fabrics.

FINISHED SIZE
42″ × 48″ (107 cm × 122 cm)

MATERIALS
Use quilting cottons 44–45″ (112–114 cm) wide

PATCHWORK FABRICS

Fabric A (mediums): 1/4–1/2 yd (25–46 cm) each of at least 10 different medium-light-toned and medium-toned predominantly bicolored small-scale and medium-scale prints (mostly dots, circles, and swirls) in dusky colors, including greens, rose, coral, lavender, and ochers; a total of approximately 3 yd (2.8 m)

Fabric B (darks): 1/4–1/2 yd (25–46 cm) each of at least 6–10 different medium-dark-toned and very dark-toned predominantly bicolored small-scale and medium-scale prints (mostly dots, circles, and swirls) in dusky colors, including greens, charcoal, lavenders, plums, and blue; a total of approximately 3 yd (2.8 m)

OTHER INGREDIENTS

Backing fabric: 2 yd (1.9 m) of desired fabric

Binding fabric: 1/2 yd (46 cm) of a gray-green and black stripe

Cotton batting: 49″ × 55″ (125 cm × 140 cm)

Quilting thread: Gray-green thread

Template: Use template A (see page 187)

CUTTING PATCHES

504 medium-toned triangles: Cut 504 template-A triangles from fabric A, cutting in sets of nine matching triangles—for a total of 56 sets.

504 dark-toned triangles: Cut 504 template-A triangles from fabric B, cutting in sets of nine matching triangles—for a total of 56 sets.

MAKING BLOCKS

Make the blocks using the seam allowance marked on the template.

56 blocks: Using a set of nine matching fabric-A triangles and a set of nine matching fabric-B triangles, make 56 blocks as shown in the block diagram. To add interest to the final quilt, use one to three matching patches from a different fabric A or different fabric B in some of the blocks.

Clay Tiles Block

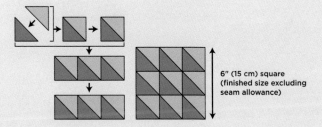

6″ (15 cm) square (finished size excluding seam allowance)

ASSEMBLING TOP

Arrange the blocks as shown on the assembly diagram (page 76), either laying them out on the floor or sticking them to a cotton-flannel design wall.

Using the seam allowance marked on the template, sew the blocks together in eight rows of seven blocks. Then sew the rows together.

Clay Tiles Assembly

KEY

Fabric A

Fabric B

FINISHING QUILT

Press the quilt top. Layer the quilt top, batting, and backing, then baste the layers together (see page 181).

Using gray-green thread, stitch-in-the-ditch around each patch.

Trim the quilt edges. Then cut the binding fabric on the bias and sew it on around the edge of the quilt (see page 181).

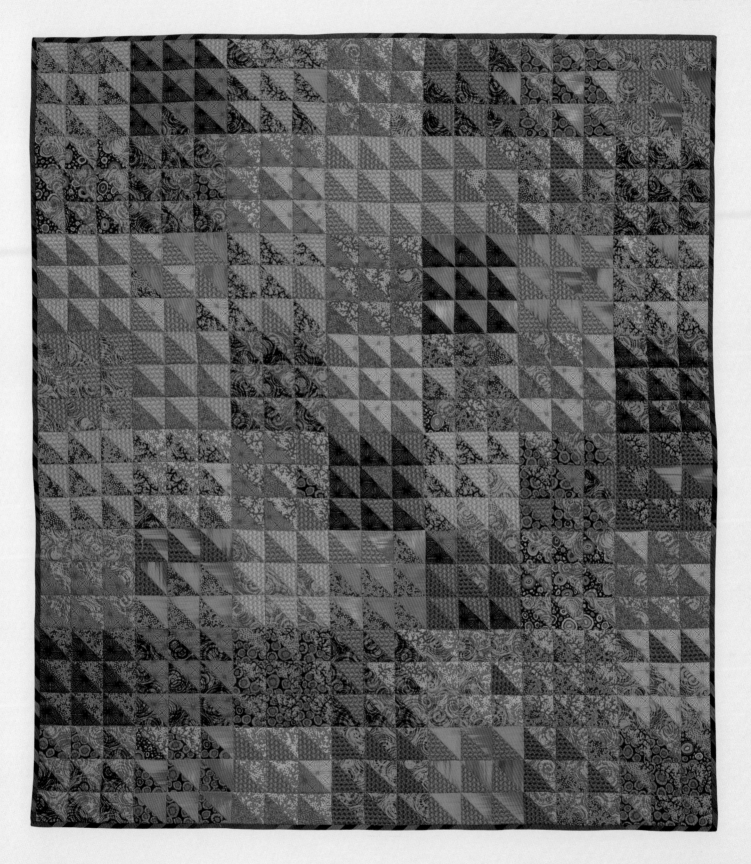

INDIGO POINTS

This simple geometry is based on Clay Tiles (page 67), but the indigo and ecru color scheme and the plain border and sashing give the composition a totally different feel. Though subtly contrasting, the triangles appear to dance within their restricted sashed framework, a movement enhanced by the dotty prints sprinkled throughout.

FINISHED SIZE

50 1/2" × 57 1/4" (128 cm × 145.5 cm)

MATERIALS

Use quilting cottons 44–45" (112–114 cm) wide

PATCHWORK FABRICS

Fabric A (lights): 1/4–1/2 yd (25–46 cm) each of at least 10 different light-toned monochromatic small-scale prints (mostly dots, circles, and florals) in ecrus, pale blues, beige, cream, off-whites, and dusty lavender; a total of approximately 3 yd (2.8 m)

Fabric B (darks): 1/4–1/2 yd (25–46 cm) each of at least 15 different medium-dark-toned and very dark-toned monochromatic small-scale and medium-scale prints (mostly dots, circles, and florals) in airforce and powder blues, indigos, gray-blues, and teal; a total of approximately 3 yd (2.8 m)

Fabric C (sashing and border fabric): 1 2/3 yd (1.5 m) of a pale lilac-blue solid—OR Kaffe Fasset *Shot Cotton* in Ice

OTHER INGREDIENTS

Backing fabric: 3 1/4 yd (3 m) of desired fabric

Binding fabric: 1/2 yd (46 cm) of a stripe

Cotton batting: 58" × 65" (145 cm × 160 cm)

Quilting thread: Gray-blue thread

Templates: Use templates A and B (see page 187)

CUTTING PATCHES

504 light-toned triangles: Cut 504 template-A triangles from fabric A, cutting in sets of nine matching triangles—for a total of 56 sets.

504 dark-toned triangles: Cut 504 template-A triangles from fabric B, cutting in sets of nine matching triangles—for a total of 56 sets.

48 short sashing strips: Cut 48 short template-B strips from fabric C.

7 long sashing strips: From fabric C, cut seven strips 47" × 1 1/4" (119.4 cm × 3.2 cm). Make sure that these strips are exactly the same width as template B.

4 border strips: From fabric C, cut two strips 2 1/2" × 47" (6.4 cm × 119.4 cm) for the top and bottom borders; then cut two strips 2 1/2" × 57 3/4" (6.4 cm × 146.7 cm) for the side borders.

MAKING BLOCKS

Make the blocks using the seam allowance marked on the templates.

56 blocks: Using a set of nine matching fabric-A triangles and a set of nine matching fabric-B triangles, make 56 blocks as shown in the block diagram. To add interest to the final quilt, use one to three matching patches from a different fabric A or different fabric B in some of the blocks.

Indigo Points Block

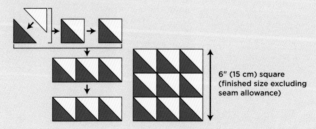

6" (15 cm) square (finished size excluding seam allowance)

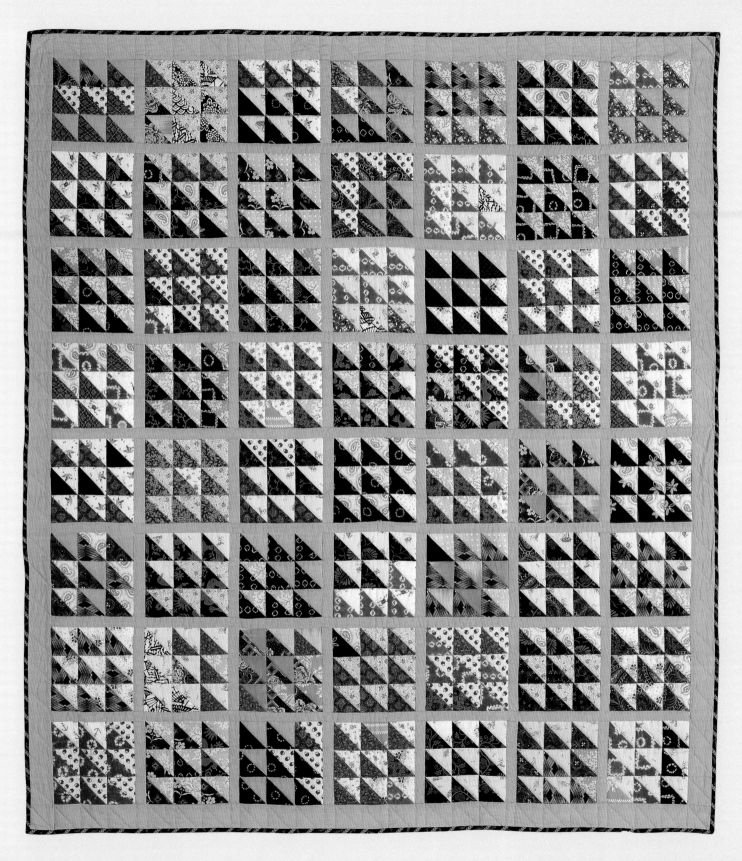

ASSEMBLING TOP

Arrange the blocks and sashing strips as shown on the assembly diagram (page 81), either laying them out on the floor or sticking them to a cotton-flannel design wall.

Using the seam allowance marked on the templates throughout, sew the blocks together in eight rows of seven blocks and six short sashing strips. Then sew the rows and long sashing strips together.

Sew the short border strips to the top and bottom of the quilt. Then sew one long border strip to each side of the quilt.

FINISHING QUILT

Press the quilt top. Layer the quilt top, batting, and backing, then baste the layers together (see page 181).

Using gray-blue thread, stitch-in-the ditch around each patch and echo this quilting pattern in the borders.

Trim the quilt edges. Then cut the binding fabric on the bias and sew it on around the edge of the quilt (see page 181).

The famous English potter Rupert Spira is always testing his beautiful range of glazes. For the test shown above, he divided triangles into delicious further triangles of various glaze recipes. They look wonderful next to the bold black–and–white stone mosaic pavings in Lisbon, Portugal (right). All this visual music underfoot makes you want to dance. Both these images are worthy of some quilt ideas, don't you think?

Indigo Points Assembly

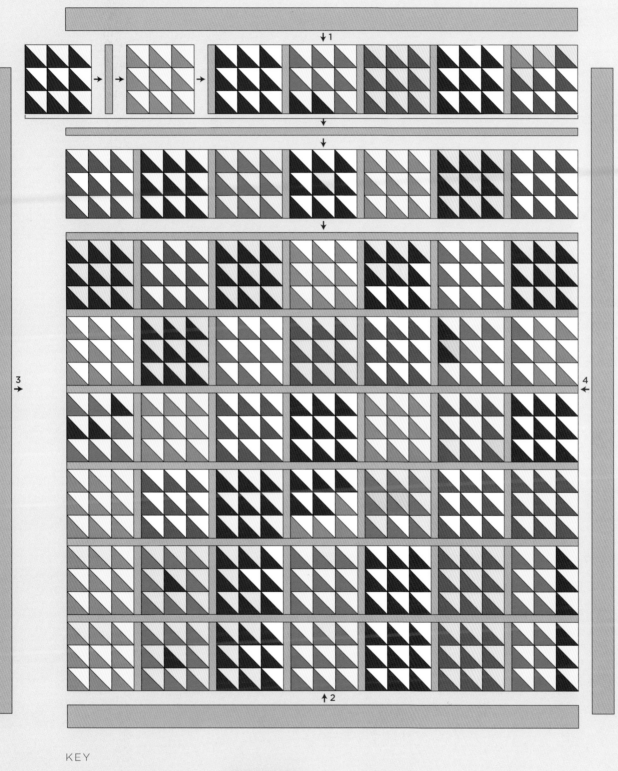

KEY

☐☐☐☐☐ Fabric A   ■■■■ Fabric B   ☐ Fabric C

EARTHY MITERED BOXES

On this quilt, striped triangles are used to form simple mitered boxes in three different sizes. All you need is three different triangle templates to cut the patches. The layout for the boxes is the same as the one for the squares on Yellow Potpourri (page 34). Once you have all the blocks made, have fun arranging and rearranging them until they form a lively composition.

FINISHED SIZE
68" × 101" (172.7 cm × 256.5 cm)

MATERIALS
Use quilting cottons 44–45" (112–114 cm) wide

PATCHWORK FABRICS

Main fabric (stripes): 1/2 yd (46 cm) each of at least 15 different broad stripes and narrow stripes in predominantly caramels, reds, fuchsias, purples, greens, and gray-blues; a total of approximately 7 1/2 yd (6.9 m)—OR 1/2 yd (46 cm) each of the following 15 Kaffe Fassett fabrics:

Bold Stripe in Gold and Fuchsia; *Multi Stripe* in Fuchsia, Purple, Indigo, and Red; *Two-toned Stripe* in Citrus, Spice, Magenta, Slate, Lavender, Moss, Suede, Purple, and Pumpkin

Inner-border fabric: 1 yd (92 cm) of a gold, red, and blue chevron stripe—OR Kaffe Fassett *Chevron Stripe* in Ochre

Outer-border fabric: 3 yd (2.8 m) of a large-scale print with violet, red, blue, and aqua motifs on a charcoal ground—OR Kaffe Fassett *Clouds* in Charcoal

OTHER INGREDIENTS

Backing fabric: 6 yd (5.6 m) of desired fabric

Binding fabric: 3/4 yd (70 cm) of a stripe

Cotton batting: 75" × 108" (190 cm × 270 cm)

Quilting thread: Medium olive thread

Templates: Use templates G, LL, and MM (see page 187)

CUTTING PATCHES

When cutting the triangle patches, align the stripes with the direction arrows on the templates—the stripes should run parallel to the longest side of each triangle. Cut each set of four almost matching triangles so that sometimes the stripes will meet up when the triangles are sewn together.

PATCHES FOR SQUARE BLOCKS

80 large triangles: From the main fabric (stripes), cut 20 sets of four matching template-G triangles—for a total of 80 triangles.

212 medium-size triangles: From the main fabric (stripes), cut 53 sets of four matching template-LL triangles—for a total of 212 triangles.

520 small triangles: From the main fabric (stripes), cut 130 sets of four matching template-G triangles—for a total of 520 triangles.

INNER BORDER

4 border strips: From the inner-border fabric, cut two strips 2 1/2" × 87 1/2" (6.4 cm × 222.3 cm) for the side borders; then cut two strips 2 1/2" × 58 1/2" (6.4 cm × 148.6 cm) for the top and bottom borders. (To make long enough strips, cut the strips selvage to selvage and sew together end to end, matching the pattern carefully.)

OUTER BORDER

4 border strips: From the outer-border fabric, cut two strips 5 1/2" × 91 1/2" (14 cm × 232.4 cm) for the side borders; then cut two strips 5 1/2" × 68 1/2" (14 cm × 174 cm) for the top and bottom borders. (To make long enough strips, cut the strips selvage to selvage and sew together end to end.)

MAKING BLOCKS

Using the seam allowance marked on the templates, sew together the blocks. To add interest to the quilt, mismatch some of the blocks by including a mismatched triangle or two in the block; you can do that by mixing up some of the block groups.

20 large mitered blocks: Using four matching triangles for each of the large square blocks, make 20 blocks as shown in the block diagram.

53 medium-size mitered blocks: Using four matching triangles for each of the medium-size square blocks, make 53 blocks as shown in the block diagram.

130 small mitered blocks: Using four matching triangles for each of the small square blocks, make 130 blocks as shown in the block diagram.

Mitered Block

  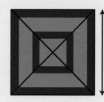

Three sizes:
3", 6", 9"
(7.6, 15.2, 22.8 cm) square
(finished sizes excluding seam allowance)

ASSEMBLING TOP

Arrange the center of the quilt in three long panels as shown on the assembly diagram for Yellow Potpourri on page 34, either laying out the mitered squares on the floor or sticking them to a cotton-flannel design wall. Take your time arranging the blocks. Sprinkle the different stripes randomly across the quilt and make sure that patches cut from the same fabric are not touching each other.

Using the seam allowance marked on the templates throughout, sew together the mitered squares. First sew the squares into three panels. For each panel, sew the squares together in sections, then sew the sections together. The bold outlines on the diagram show how to divide each panel into sections and avoid inset seams. After the panels have been stitched together, sew the panels together.

Stitch the four inner border strips to the quilt center, sewing on the long side strips first and then the short top and bottom strips. Lastly, stitch the four outer border strips to the quilt center, sewing on the long side strips first and then the short top and bottom strips.

When my sister Kim, who loves to sew, visited me in London one year we set about making this circus of a quilt in a squares format similar to that of Earthy Mitered Boxes. We didn't let stripes intimidate us and we quite deliberately mixed up the squares to achieve a happy discord. The primitive contrasts delighted us.

FINISHING QUILT

Press the quilt top. Layer the quilt top, batting, and backing, then baste the layers together (see page 181).

Using medium olive thread, stitch-in-the-ditch around the patches in the quilt center. Then machine-quilt the borders, outlining the chevrons on the inner border and the motifs in the outer border.

Trim the quilt edges. Then cut the binding fabric on the bias and sew it on around the edge of the quilt (see page 181).

During one of my many walks around London I came upon an old Victorian cemetery that featured some grand memorial buildings, including this one with such a gorgeous patina. The stone surfaces made a perfect setting for the natural colors in Earthy Mitered Boxes.

DIAMONDS

It is challenging to find diamonds in everyday life but, occasionally, while I am walking around in London, I see diamond shapes created with contrasting brick colors on Edwardian and later buildings. Decorative diamond designs on iron manhole covers also catch my attention during my walks. In gardens I spot latticework trellises studded with negative diamond shapes. So they are to be discovered if you are really looking.

My favorite diamonds are found on the stickwork shelters in old English country gardens. These rustic garden houses, which speak of a time when people wanted a bit of decorative fancywork around to light up their passage through life, are often covered with dense geometric designs constructed of rows of thin branches nailed onto the walls. And sometimes these quaint shelters are filled with benches and tables in the same hypnotic stickwork.

The floors and pavings under your feet are another place to look for scintillating diamonds. Ancient pebble mosaics in continental Europe abound with diamonds, the simple geometry softened by the knobby texture. The pattern on the smooth tiled floor on page 87 (bottom right) has inspired my knitting, needlepoint, and fabric designs. What a sense of movement is created by the squares and diamonds dancing through that amazing concoction. Mosaics are another happy medium for diamonds. At the entrance to our London house my assistant Brandon made a bold diamonds mosaic, creating pools of colors with broken tiles and dishes. It breaks up our boring porch delightfully and is a joy to come home to see (page 108).

While writing these words, I was contacted by my yarn company and asked to revive the argyle motif in my next collection of knit patterns, as argyles are all the rage in fashion just now. I looked at Bordered Diamonds (page 95) and thought that patchwork format would make a great new variation on the traditional argyle. So, I have knitted up a very colorful field of diamonds with contrasting borders. Of course, the diamond shape progresses as naturally and effortlessly in weaving as it does in knitting, which makes it an easy shape with which to improvise. I have a collection of colorful knitted Peruvian hats and African textiles that use diamonds in deliciously inventive ways.

And what an elegant shape the diamond presents in so many of the classic quilt layouts! Tumbling blocks and stars are fancy uses of the diamond in quilts, so eye-catching even when done in monochromatic palettes. I like the way rows of florals in diamond shapes slot into each other. Each diamond in its row juts into the row of diamonds below, mixing the pattern surface up in a wonderfully energetic way. Diamonds also make delicious borders on quilts, as you can see in any book on vintage English quilts.

My antique lozenge quilt (page 86, top left) uses the geometry of diamonds in an unexpected way. I love to study it carefully, marveling at the fussy-cut symmetry of the piecing. The sensitive coloring and jazzy use of stripes are just a couple of its wonders. How amazing it is that those simple tiny hexagons pieced together add up to such refined diamond shapes. The intricacy of small-piece quilts like this one fascinates me, mainly because I can't imagine spending the weeks and possibly years it takes to make them. But, thankfully, someone had the patience to create these masterpieces for us to enjoy.

Cutting diamonds from prints and juxtaposing them to create six-pointed stars is a great chance to fussy-cut motifs and play with directional stripes within the simple shapes. The effect is kaleidoscopic on Circle of Stars (opposite page, bottom). On the other hand, splitting each diamond on eight-pointed stars, as on this tiled wall in Portugal (opposite page, top), adds a slender elegance to them that would make a smart mariner's compass on a quilt layout. The emboldened diamonds on this knitted Peruvian hat (above) were the inspiration for Bordered Diamonds on page 95.

CIRCLE OF STARS

I found this fabulous patchwork layout, in which all of the intriguing shapes are made from one-size diamond patches, in a book on antique Australian quilts. The original was done in beiges and dark browns, so I tickled up the palette just a tad. You need contrast between stars to create the circular movement. But it could also be done with very soft pastels and closer tones—think of sugared almonds and Easter eggs.

For this colorway, I was thinking of the costumes in Comedia Del Arte: bright eye-catching colors with more muted ochers, browns, and deep burgundys. I particularly like the balance of solid and patterned fabrics. When it came time to photograph this quilt, a large, dark brick arch that supports our local railway made our palette sing, and the powerful curves spoke to that circle of stars magnificently.

See instructions on pages 98–105.

FACET

Like Haze Kilim (page 66), Facet was inspired by one of my knitwear designs, in this case a commissioned jacket with long, striped diamond motifs. To emulate the look of knitted stripes in patchwork, Liza encouraged me to use a string-piecing technique.

The trick to choosing the many fabrics needed to create these large contrasting diamonds is to stick with fabrics with enough similar colors to create a solid mass of the tone you want—dark or light—while also being sure to let in some with spicy variations.

During one of my many walks seeking out locations to shoot the finished quilts for this book, I found this Victorian storefront with gray and maroon peeling paint. When I returned on the day of the shoot, scaffolding with red-and-white tape on it had been erected. Initially taken aback, I ultimately decided that these new additions contributed to the general gaiety of the scene.
See instructions on pages 106–110.

◀ BORDERED DIAMONDS

Flipping through a textile magazine, I noticed a photo of the back of a paper-pieced diamond patchwork. The colored paper shapes surrounded by fabric borders covering the front of each diamond inspired me to take all my newest big florals and edge them in small textured prints in a contrasting palette. This version is biased toward a hot red palette with blue and purple notes and gold highlights. Doesn't it look radiant on the scarlet walls of a Brazilian restaurant in north London? A very graphic version with solid diamonds and prints on the borders like my original inspiration would also work well, as would a variation with few colors, for example, all black background florals with just four alternating small print borders.

See instructions on pages 116–119.

◀ ST. MARKS

Whenever I visit St. Marks Cathedral in Venice, I am awestruck by the wild inventiveness of all the different mosaic patterns in the marble floors, made all the more beautiful by the soft, rich patina of age. So, when Liza proposed this quilt as soon as we committed to a chapter on diamonds, I was immediately captivated. She drew out the proportions and we started choosing fabrics. They had to be contrasting but soft like old stone, so we tried to find darks with rich medium tones and lights with a slight warming effect on the cool silveriness of it all.

See instructions on pages 111–115.

NOT-SO-LONE STAR

*Ever since I saw a particularly bold lone-star quilt
designed by my friend Claudia, I've wanted to
try my own daring variation, so here it is (with a
few extra stars at the corners, thus its name). I've
noticed that most quilters choose off-white or, at
best, solid-colored backgrounds for their large-
star quilts, so whenever I see one where the quilter
let it rip and placed her dynamic star on a strong
patterned fabric, it feels like a special treat! I made
mine with one of my boldest prints, called* Lake
Blossoms, *in a good, dark colorway. The lighter
colors contrast to create quite a buzz. You could
do a deeper-colored star for a more subtle effect.
Send me a picture if you do.*

*I do look forward to seeing the variations you
quilters will get up to, but I hope you always have
a strong big-scale background, which to me is the
cornerstone of the design.*

See instructions on pages 120–125.

CIRCLE OF STARS

With its many diamond patches, inset seams, and rings of stars, this is not a quilt for a beginner. But the experienced quilter with advanced stitching skills will definitely enjoy the challenge. The hard work is worth the effort—a quilt that is a true heirloom masterpiece. The instructions are laid out carefully to make the process of assembly as easy as possible.

FINISHED SIZE
88" × 108" (223.5 cm × 274 cm)

MATERIALS
Use quilting cottons 44–45" (112–114 cm) wide

PATCHWORK FABRICS

Fabric A: 1/2 yd (46 cm) of a subtle dark-toned stripe in raspberry

Fabric B: 1/2 yd (46 cm) of a medium-toned print in gray, blue, and pink

Fabric C: 1 yd (92 cm) of a medium-toned solid in chartreuse—OR Kaffe Fassett *Shot Cotton* in Chartreuse

Fabric D: 1/2 yd (46 cm) of a dark-toned print in lavender, puce, and green

Fabric E: 1/2 yd (46 cm) of a light-medium-toned print in brown, caramel, and black

Fabric F: 1/2 yd (46 cm) of a medium-toned solid in veridian green—OR Kaffe Fassett *Shot Cotton* in Veridian

Fabric G: 1/4 yd (25 cm) of a dark-toned print in navy, blue, and red

Fabric H: 1 yd (92 cm) of a subtle dark-toned stripe in burgundy

Fabric J: 1/2 yd (46 cm) of a light-medium-toned print in green, moss, and blue

Fabric K: 1 yd (92 cm) of a light-medium-toned solid in vermillion red—OR Kaffe Fassett *Shot Cotton* in Vermillion

Fabric L: 1/2 yd (46 cm) of a medium-toned print in green, moss, and orange

Fabric M: 1 1/4 yd (1.2 m) of a light-medium-toned solid in tobacco brown—OR Kaffe Fassett *Shot Cotton* in Tobacco

Fabric N: 1/2 yd (46 cm) of a light-toned print in periwinkle, raspberry, and aqua

Fabric O: 1/2 yd (46 cm) of a subtle dark-toned stripe in lavender

Fabric P: 1/2 yd (46 cm) of a light-toned print in dusky lilac, gold, and aqua

Fabric Q: 1/2 yd (46 cm) of a medium-toned mini print in dusky brown and green

Fabric R: 1/2 yd (46 cm) of a light-toned print in lavender, pink, and aqua

Fabric S: 1/2 yd (46 cm) of a dark-toned print in orange and red

Fabric T: 1 yd (92 cm) of a light-toned solid in jade green—OR Kaffe Fassett *Shot Cotton* in Jade

Fabric U: 1/2 yd (46 cm) of a light-medium-toned subtle stripe in orange

Fabric V: 1/2 yd (46 cm) of a dark-toned print in burgundy and moss

Fabric W: 1 yd (92 cm) of a light-toned print in moss green

Fabric X: 1 yd (92 cm) of a dark-toned solid in brick red—OR Kaffe Fassett *Shot Cotton* in Brick

Fabric Y: 1/2 yd (46 cm) of a medium-toned print in green, fuchsia, and gold

Fabric Z: 1 yd (92 cm) of a light-toned solid in blue—OR Kaffe Fassett *Shot Cotton* in Forget-Me-Not Blue

Fabric AA: 1/2 yd (46 cm) of a dark-toned print in red, black, and fuchsia

Fabric BB: 1/2 yd (46 cm) of a light-medium-toned print in blue, lavender, and aqua

Fabric CC: 1 yd (92 cm) of a subtle dark-toned stripe in purple

Fabric DD: 1/2 yd (46 cm) of a light-medium-toned mini print in blue

Fabric EE: 1/2 yd (46 cm) of a subtle medium-toned stripe in fuchsia

Fabric FF: 1 yd (92 cm) of a solid in black—OR Kaffe Fassett *Shot Cotton* in Coal

OTHER INGREDIENTS

Backing fabric: 9 yd (8.3 m) of desired fabric

Binding fabric: 1 yd (92 cm) of a small-scale print in charcoal

Cotton batting: 95" × 115" (240 cm × 290 cm)

Quilting thread: Sage-green thread

Templates: Use templates H, J, K, and L (see pages 188 and 189)

SPECIAL FABRIC NOTE

Pay particular attention to the suggested "tone" for each of the 31 fabrics needed for the quilt. No matter how close in tone the fabrics are, there needs to be enough contrast in lightness and darkness (or in sharp color contrast) for the stars to stand out against their individual backgrounds and for each block to stand out against its neighbor so that the blocks will form distinct rings of color. Notice in particular how the fourth ring of stars from the center pops out because it uses lighter fabrics than all the other rings; the background fabrics for this ring of bordered stars (fabrics T and W) don't have to be *very* light, but they need to be distinctly lighter than the backgrounds in the other rings.

If you are using the suggested Kaffe Fassett *Shot Cotton* fabrics for the eight solid-colored fabrics in this quilt, purchase these first (fabrics C, F, K, M, T, X, Z, and FF) so that you have them on hand when choosing the remaining fabrics. Select small-scale and medium-scale prints and choose fabrics for their color, not for their pattern appeal since the pieces are all cut quite small.

CUTTING PATCHES

There are two types of stars in the quilt and they alternate—bordered stars and hexagon stars. Follow the instructions carefully, using the table and diagrams provided while cutting patches, making blocks, arranging blocks, and assembling the quilt.

QUILT STARS

These are the patches you will need to cut for each of the two types of stars:

Hexagon star block: For the center-star, cut six template-H diamonds for the star. For the background, cut four template-H diamonds and four small template-J triangles. (See the Hexagon Star Block diagram on page 101.)

Bordered star: For the center-star, cut six template-H diamonds. For the background, cut four template-H diamonds, four small template-J triangles, and six large template-K triangles. (See the pieces of Bordered Star diagram on page 101. Note that the bordered star at each outer corner of the quilt requires only five large template-K triangles instead of the usual six.)

Start at the center of the quilt and cut the pieces needed for the bordered star at the very center, using the fabrics listed in the Rings Table (page 102) for the center-star patches and the background patches.

Next, cut the patches for the first ring of hexagon stars (ring 1) around the center bordered star (see the diagram for the arrangement of rings of stars on page 103). There are a total of six stars in ring 1. Use the fabrics listed in the Rings Table, cutting the patches for three of the stars in one colorway and the patches for the remaining three stars in the second colorway. Where there are two fabrics listed for the center-star, cut three of the six diamonds needed for the star in one fabric and the remaining three in the other fabric.

Continue in this way, working your way outward and cutting the patches for each ring of stars before proceeding to the next. It is a good idea to work on a large cotton-flannel design wall when making this quilt. You can then stick the patches on the wall as you cut them. (If you are doing this, follow the arrangement diagram for the placement of the rings of stars and the assembly diagram on page 105 for the positioning of the colorways in each ring.)

EDGE TRIANGLES

Once you have cut the patches for all the rings of stars, cut the edge triangles as follows:

6 template-K triangles: From fabric FF, cut six template-K triangles to fill in the edges at the sides of the quilt.

12 template-L triangles: From fabric FF, cut 12 template-L triangles to fill in the edges at the top and bottom of the quilt.

MAKING BLOCKS

Make the blocks using the seam allowance marked on the templates.

Hexagon star blocks: Using the patches cut for each of the hexagon stars in rings 1, 3, 5, and 7, sew each block together as shown in the block diagram.

Hexagon Star Block

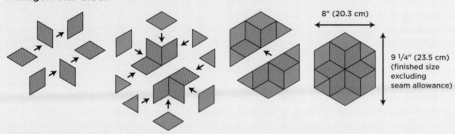

8" (20.3 cm)

9 1/4" (23.5 cm) (finished size excluding seam allowance)

Bordered stars: Using the patches cut for each of the bordered stars—including the star at the very center of the quilt, those in rings 2, 4, 6, and the four quilt corner stars—sew together the hexagon block at the center of each of the bordered stars. But DO NOT sew on the six large template-K triangles that complete the borders. These triangles are sewn on when the quilt is assembled in diagonal rows.

Pieces of Bordered Star

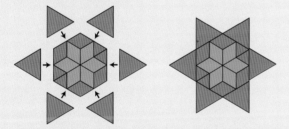

ARRANGING STARS

If you have not kept the blocks arranged on your design wall, you should arrange them now. Arrange them in the rings shown on the arrangement diagram (page 103), either laying out the stars (and the loose patches of the bordered stars) on the floor or sticking them to a cotton-flannel design wall.

Start by positioning the bordered star at the very center of the quilt, positioning the template-K triangles around the block to complete the background border. Following the arrangement diagram, position each ring of stars around the center, starting with ring 1 and working outward. Note that the arrangement diagram shows the positions of the rings but not the fabric colors. Look at the assembly diagram for the positions of the various star colorways in each ring.

Lastly, position the edge triangles to make the edges straight along the sides and top and bottom of the quilt. The four template-L triangles at the corners along the top and bottom of the quilt will be too long, so trim them to fit as you assemble the quilt.

In this design the color does the work of separating the richly patterned stars from their large diamond borders. When quilting a pattern as complex as this one, it is very important to use a thread color that melts into the patchwork. These stars could be done in more traditional small prints and a softer palette for a more conservative look.

The Industrial Revolution brought us some grand old designs—functional machinery in distinctive forms. These cast-iron wheels are splendid inspiration with their deep rust patinas and circle diamond shapes, basic geometry you can see echoed in Circle of Stars.

Rings Table for Circle of Stars

This table gives the fabrics used for the bordered stars and the hexagon stars in the quilt. Follow this table and the Arrangement of Rings of Stars diagram when cutting the patches and arranging the blocks.

	NUMBER OF STARS	CENTER-STAR FABRIC/S	BACKGROUND FABRIC
Center	1 Bordered Star	Fabric B	Fabric A
Ring 1	3 Hexagon Stars	Fabric D	Fabric C
	3 Hexagon Stars	Fabrics F and G	Fabric E
Ring 2	3 Bordered Stars	Fabric J	Fabric H
	3 Bordered Stars	Fabric L	Fabric K
Ring 3	6 Hexagon Stars	Fabric N	Fabric M
	6 Hexagon Stars	Fabric P	Fabric O
	6 Hexagon Stars	Fabrics R and S	Fabric Q
Ring 4	6 Bordered Stars	Fabrics U and V	Fabric T
	6 Bordered Stars	Fabric B	Fabric W
Ring 5	9 Hexagon Stars	Fabric S	Fabric C
	12 Hexagon Stars	Fabrics Y and Z	Fabric X
	9 Hexagon Stars	Fabrics AA and BB	Fabric C
Ring 6*	8 Bordered Stars	Fabric E	Fabric CC
	8 Bordered Stars	Fabric D	Fabric K
Ring 7*	4 Hexagon Stars	Fabric N	Fabric A
	9 Hexagon Stars	Fabric U	Fabric F
	9 Hexagon Stars	Fabric EE	Fabric DD
Corners	4 Bordered Stars	Fabric B	Fabric M

*Note: The hexagon stars in rings 6 and 7 do not go all the way around the quilt like the stars in the other rings (see the Arrangement of Rings of Stars diagram).

KEY

- Center Star
- Star Ring 1
- Star Ring 2
- Star Ring 3
- Star Ring 4
- Star Ring 5
- Star Ring 6
- Star Ring 7
- Corner Stars

Arrangement of Rings of Stars

ASSEMBLING TOP

With the blocks and patches arranged in their correct position, you are now ready to sew them together.

Using the seam allowance marked on the templates throughout, sew the blocks and patches together in diagonal rows as shown on the assembly diagram. Be sure to keep the pieces in place on the floor or design wall until you need them because assembling the diagonal rows is tricky; you will see that the template-K triangles are not always sewn to their own star but to a neighboring star to complete the bordered effect. Once each of the diagonal rows is sewn together, sew the diagonal rows to each other to complete the quilt top.

FINISHING QUILT

Press the quilt top. Layer the quilt top, batting, and backing, then baste the layers together (see page 181).

Using sage-green thread, machine-echo-quilt 1/4" (6 mm) inside the outer edge of each diamond in each star and inside the outer edge of each bordered hexagon. Stitch-in-the-ditch around each hexagon at the center of each bordered star. Lastly, machine-quilt meandering lines in the backgrounds of the hexagon stars (not in the backgrounds of the bordered stars).

Trim the quilt edges. Then cut the binding fabric on the bias and sew it on around the edge of the quilt (see page 181).

KEY

■	Fabric A	□	Fabric R
■	Fabric B	■	Fabric S
■	Fabric C	■	Fabric T
■	Fabric D	■	Fabric U
■	Fabric E	■	Fabric V
■	Fabric F	■	Fabric W
■	Fabric G	■	Fabric X
■	Fabric H	■	Fabric Y
■	Fabric J	■	Fabric Z
■	Fabric K	■	Fabric AA
■	Fabric L	■	Fabric BB
■	Fabric M	■	Fabric CC
■	Fabric N	■	Fabric DD
■	Fabric O	■	Fabric EE
□	Fabric P	■	Fabric FF
■	Fabric Q		

Circle of Stars Assembly

FACET

This quilt is made using the traditional technique called string piecing. Long scrap strips (strings) are sewn together to make new, pieced material and the triangle patches for the quilt are cut from the new material. This same technique is used for Haze Kilim (page 66).

FINISHED SIZE
72" × 72" (183 cm × 183 cm)

MATERIALS
Use quilting cottons 44–45" (112–114 cm) wide

PATCHWORK FABRICS

Fabric A (lights): A large assortment of light-toned fabric scraps, including mostly multicolored floral and circular motif prints of any scale, plus some stripes, checks, and polka dots; all in ranges of pinks, oranges, blues, and moss greens—the scraps should be at least 11" (28 cm) long

Fabric B (darks): A large assortment of dark-toned fabric scraps, including mostly multicolored floral and circular motif prints of any scale, plus some stripes, checks, and polka dots; all in ranges of purples, reds, browns, and greens—the scraps should be at least 11" (28 cm) long

Fabric C (border): 1 1/4 yd (1.2 m) of a chevron stripe or a diagonal stripe in fuchsia, pink, red, cinnamon, and purple—OR Kaffe Fassett *Chevron Stripes* in Red

OTHER INGREDIENTS

Backing fabric: 5 yd (4.6 m) of desired fabric

Binding fabric: 3/4 yd (70 cm) of a dark-toned small-scale circles print

Cotton batting: 79" × 79" (200 cm × 200 cm)

Quilting thread: Taupe thread

PREPARING STRING-PIECED FABRICS

All the big triangle patches for the quilt top are cut from string-pieced fabrics. Preparing the fabrics takes time, and you will get the best results if you don't rush. Note that the prepared string-pieced rectangles are bigger than necessary, so you don't need to pay too much attention to lining the strips up precisely when stitching them together—there is more than 2" (5 cm) extra both widthwise and lengthwise in each string-pieced rectangle; they will be trimmed once starched and pressed.

CUTTING AND SORTING

Cut all fabrics into strips 11" (28 cm) long and in random widths—1 1/4–3" (3–7.5 cm) wide. Keep the light (fabric-A) strips together and the dark (fabric-B) strips together.

Sort the light strips (fabric-A strips) into four groups of similar colors—pinks, oranges, blues, and greens. These are only guidelines because the fabrics are multicolored and the groups will not look totally a single color. Each group will be sewn together to make a new "fabric," so take your time in selecting the strips for each group. Some colors can be used in two groups, but keep the overall look of the four groups predominantly pinks, oranges, blues, and greens.

Next sort the dark strips (fabric-B strips) into four groups of similar colors—purples, reds, browns, and greens. Sort them in the same way as for the light strips, keeping the overall look of the four groups predominantly purples, reds, browns, and greens, but overlapping some colors into two groups.

PIECING STRIPS INTO 32 RECTANGLES

Take the "pink" group of light strips and lay them out in four random arrangements, aligning the strips side by side. Using a 1/4" (6 mm) seam allowance and stitching along the long edges of the strips, sew together the strips in each "pink" arrangement to make four separate rectangles of pieced strips. The finished rectangles should each measure 11" (28 cm) wide (the length of the strips) by at least 20" (51 cm) long, with the stripes running widthwise.

Wanting to spruce up our London entryway, my assistant Brandon created this primitive diamond design, which has an effect similar to Facet. He smashed up garage-sale and flea-market finds with gay abandon and filled each diamond shape with pools of a certain color. He loves the teapot spouts and cup handles so they are dotted about. The door color is listed as Revenge!

Make four rectangles from each of the remaining three groups of the fabric-A strips (lights) in the same way. You should have a total of 16 fabric-A rectangles, each 11" (28 cm) wide by at least 20" (51 cm) long, with the stripes running widthwise.

Make a total of 16 rectangles from the fabric-B strips (darks) in the same way, making four rectangles from each of the four color groups.

PRESSING AND STARCHING

Press all the seams open on each of the 32 pieced rectangles. Then starch the sheets with a strong starch to make the fabric as stiff as possible and press again. Many of the seams on this quilt are sewn along the slanting edges, so it is important to use a strong starch and to make an effort to keep the pieced rectangles and the cut pieces flat until they are all sewn together.

TRIMMING RECTANGLES

Trim all the 32 starched rectangles to measure *exactly* 8 5/8" (21.9 cm) wide by 17 5/16" (44 cm) long.

CUTTING PATCHES

32 light-toned triangles: Cut eight of the 8 5/8" (21.9 cm) by 17 5/16" (44 cm) light-toned rectangles from corner to corner diagonally as shown in the first cutting diagram; then cut the remaining eight from corner to corner diagonally in the OPPOSITE DIRECTION as shown in the second cutting diagram—for a total of 32 large light-toned triangles.

32 dark-toned triangles: Cut eight of the 8 5/8" (21.9 cm) by 17 5/16" (44 cm) dark-toned rectangles from corner to corner diagonally as shown in the first cutting diagram; then cut the remaining eight from corner to corner diagonally in the OPPOSITE DIRECTION as shown in the second cutting diagram—for a total of 32 large dark-toned triangles.

Cutting the String-Pieced Rectangles

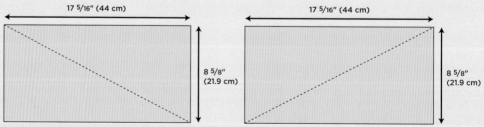

Cut eight light string-pieced and eight dark string-pieced rectangles like this.

Cut eight light string-pieced and eight dark string-pieced rectangles like this.

Facet Assembly

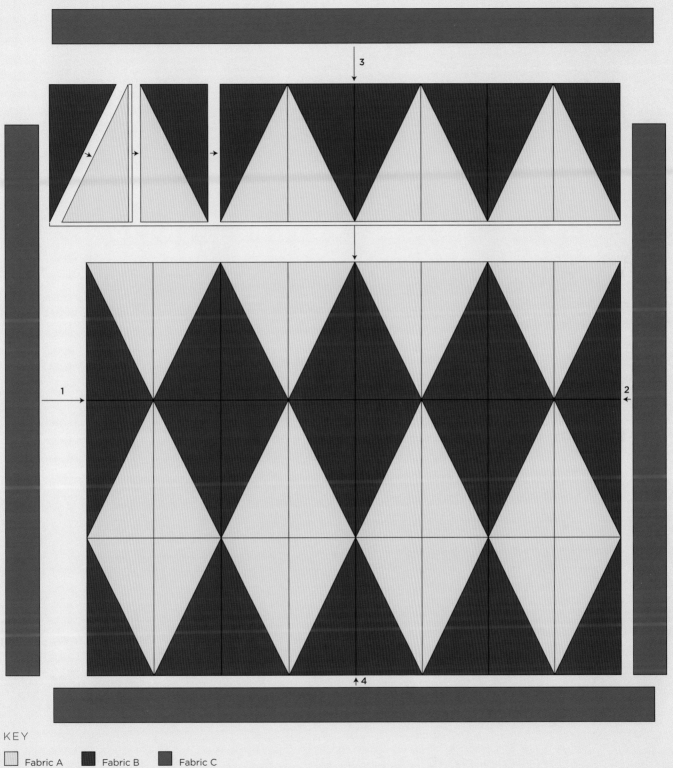

KEY

☐ Fabric A   ■ Fabric B   ■ Fabric C

My Chevron Stripes fabric makes a great border for this quilt, which we shot against scaffolding pipes with diagonal tape stripes on them. It is a joy to see the way the scrap fabrics in the diamonds blend together to create a tone of color. Note how the large assembled diamonds are emphasized by the echo quilting that repeats the shape.

4 border strips: From fabric C, cut two strips 4 1/2" (11.4 cm) by 64 1/2" (163.8 cm) for the side borders; then cut two strips 4 1/2" (11.4 cm) by 72 1/2" (184.2 cm) for the top and bottom borders. If you are using the suggested Kaffe Fassett fabric, cut the two strips from selvage to selvage for each border strip and sew them together end to end, matching the stripes carefully. Cut the border strips to the correct lengths from these pieced strips, centering a chevron in the middle of each border. If you are using a diagonal stripe, you can carefully piece strips together to create the chevron effect.

ASSEMBLING TOP

Arrange the quilt center as shown on the assembly diagram (page 109), either laying out the patches on the floor or sticking them to a cotton-flannel design wall. Arrange the triangles to form the alternating light and dark diamond shapes.
Be careful not to position two triangles from the same color group side by side in a diamond.

Using a 1/4" (6 mm) seam allowance throughout, sew the triangle patches together in pairs to form rectangles, then sew the rectangles together in horizontal rows. Lastly, sew the four horizontal rows together.

Sew the side borders to the center quilt, then sew on the top and bottom borders.

FINISHING QUILT

Press the quilt top. Layer the quilt top, batting, and backing, then baste the layers together (see page 181).

Using taupe thread, stitch-in-the ditch around the patches. Then inside each big diamond machine-stitch five concentric diamond shapes echoing the big diamonds; these diamond shapes should be about 1 1/4" (3 cm) apart, starting 1 1/4" (3 cm) from the outer edge of the big diamond and getting smaller and smaller toward the center of the diamond. Machine-stitch long lines in the border echoing the chevrons.

Trim the quilt edges. Then cut the binding fabric on the bias and sew it on around the edge of the quilt (see page 181).

ST. MARKS

The fabrics for this quilt were chosen to resemble stone, marble, and granite colors. You can use up your own scraps, including these same hues, to achieve a very similar look. Be sure to choose lots of prints with circular motifs to imitate the circular and swirling markings on granite and marble. To achieve the three-dimensional effect, sort your tones carefully.

FINISHED SIZE
63 1/4" × 80" (160.5 cm × 203 cm)

MATERIALS
Use quilting cottons 44–45" (112–114 cm) wide

PATCHWORK FABRICS

Fabric A (darks): 1/4 yd (25 cm) each of at least six different dark-toned small-scale and medium-scale circular florals in browns, gray-blues, and other earthy darks; a total of approximately 1 1/2 yd (1.4 m)—OR 1/4 yd (25 cm) each of the six following Rowan fabrics:

Aboriginal Dots in Olive; *Clover* in Black; *Daisy* in Black; *Ivy* in Teal; *Lichen* in Brown; and *Stencil Carnation* in Olive

Fabric B (mediums): 1/4 yd (25 cm) each of at least 10 different medium-toned medium-scale polka dots and medium-scale and large-scale circular floral and leaf prints in gray-blues, gray-greens, pinky browns, and other medium-toned granites; a total of approximately 2 1/2 yd (2.3 m)—OR 1/4 yd (25 cm) each of the 10 following Rowan fabrics:

Aboriginal Dots in Grey; *Begonia Leaves* in Natural; *Heraldic* in Opal; *Ikat Dots* in Sage; *Lichen* in Ochre; *Paperweight* in Sludge; *Spot* in Chocolate, Ice, and Slate; and *Stencil Carnation* in Taupe

Fabric C (lights): 1/4–1/2 yd (25–46 cm) each of at least 10 different pale-toned and light-toned medium-scale florals in browny pinks, aquas, corals, and grayed creams; a total of approximately 3 3/4 yd (3.5 m)—OR the 10 following Rowan fabrics:

1/2 yd (46 cm) each of *Aboriginal Dots* in Mint, Cream, and Sweet Pea; *Ivy* in Grey; and *Winding Floral* in Pastel

1/4 yd (25 cm) each of *Aboriginal Dots* in Ivory; *Clover* in Lilac, Grey, and Mint; and *Paperweight* in Pastel

Fabric D (light-mediums): 1/2 yd (46 cm) each of two different light-medium-toned large-scale prints in dusky turquoise, pink, and gray-green—OR 1/2 yd (46 cm) each of the two following Rowan fabrics:

Lichen in Celadon; and *Turkish Delight* in Grey

Fabric E: 1 yd (92 cm) of a medium-toned medium-scale speckled mid-gray print with pink and blue accents—OR 1 yd (92 cm) of Rowan *Guinea Flower* in White

OTHER INGREDIENTS

Backing fabric: 5 yd (4.6 m) of desired fabric

Binding fabric: 3/4 yd (70 cm) extra of one of the fabric-A prints

Cotton batting: 71" × 87" (175 cm × 220 cm)

Quilting thread: Light-medium gray thread

Templates: Use templates A, B, C, and D (see page 190)

CUTTING PATCHES

There are 59 blocks in the quilt center. Each block is made up of nine template-A diamonds. Around the edges of the blocks are some extra strips of diamonds that complete the pattern. The edging triangles are all cut from the same fabric (fabric E).

BLOCK PATCHES

59 fabric-A diamonds (darks): Cut 59 template-A diamonds from fabric A.

177 fabric-B diamonds (mediums): Cut 59 sets of three matching template-A diamonds from fabric B—for a total of 177 diamonds.

236 fabric-C diamonds (lights): Cut 59 sets of four matching template-A diamonds from fabric C—for a total of 236 diamonds.

This is my gorgeous, subtle antique lozenge quilt. I could look and look and look at this soft undemonstrative statement, it is bestowed with so many delightful qualities. The careful selection of prints never becomes brash or outspoken, yet is so playful. Notice the stripes and how jauntily they are laid out twisting this way and that like pretty ribbons fluttering on the summer breeze. St. Marks has a kindred diamond spirit, with the dot prints evoking the delicate roundness of the tiny hexagon patches in the vintage patchwork.

59 fabric-D diamonds (light-mediums): Cut 59 template-A diamonds from fabric D.

DIAMOND STRIPS

44 fabric-C diamonds (lights): Cut 22 matching pairs of template-A diamonds from fabric C—for a total of 44 patches.

23 fabric-D diamonds (light-mediums): Cut 23 template-A diamonds from fabric D.

EDGING PATCHES

12 top and bottom edging-triangles: Cut 12 template-B triangles from fabric E.

8 side edging-triangles: Cut eight template-C triangles from fabric E.

4 corner edging-triangles: Cut two template-D triangles and two template-D-reverse triangles from fabric E—for a total of four corner triangles.

MAKING BLOCKS

Make the blocks using the seam allowance marked on the templates.

59 diamond blocks: For each of the 59 diamond blocks, sew together one fabric-A (dark) diamond, three matching fabric-B (medium-toned) diamonds, four matching fabric-C (light-toned) diamonds, and one fabric-D (light-medium-toned) diamond as shown in the block diagram.

Diamond Block

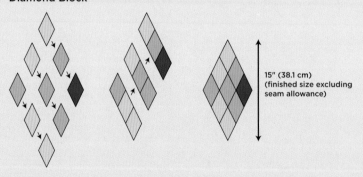

15" (38.1 cm) (finished size excluding seam allowance)

22 diamond strips: For each of the *first 11 strips*, sew together two matching fabric-C (light-toned) diamonds, then add one fabric-D (light-medium-toned) diamond at the end of the strip as for the three-patch strips along the bottom edge of the quilt next to the large edging triangles as shown on the diagram on page 114. Then for each of the *remaining 11 strips*, sew together two matching fabric-C (light-toned) diamonds, then add one fabric-D (light-medium-toned) diamond at the end of the strip as for the three-patch strips along the top edge of the quilt next to the large edging triangles—these are mirror images of the first set of strips as they slant in the opposite direction. Take one of the last strips and add an extra fabric-D (light-medium-toned) diamond at the opposite end of the pair of light patches. You should now have 21 three-patch diamond strips and one four-patch diamond strip.

St. Marks Assembly

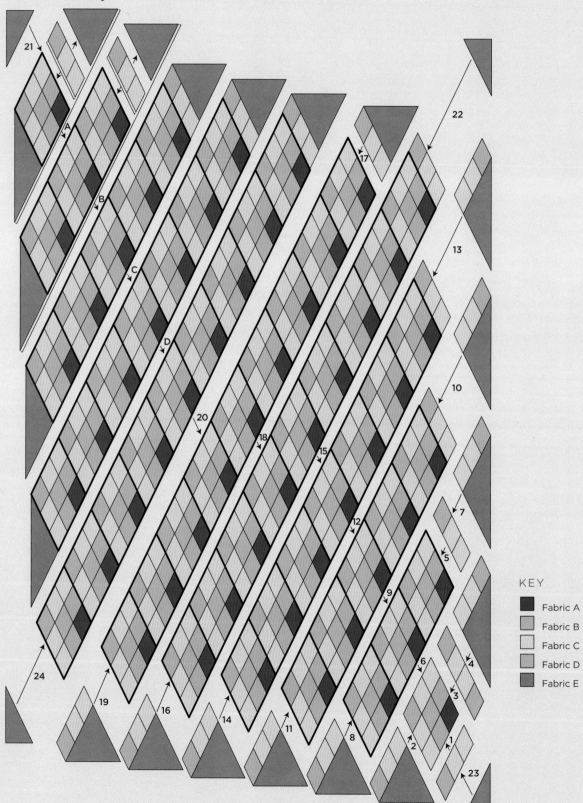

KEY

■ Fabric A
■ Fabric B
□ Fabric C
■ Fabric D
■ Fabric E

ASSEMBLING TOP

Arrange the blocks as shown on the assembly diagram (page 114), either laying them out on the floor or sticking them to a cotton-flannel design wall. For the top of the quilt center, position a horizontal row of seven diamond blocks, then add a horizontal row of six diamond blocks that nestle in between the first row of diamonds. Continue in this way, adding a row of seven blocks and six blocks alternately, until you have five rows of seven blocks and four rows of six blocks.

Next arrange the three-patch diamond strips along the top, right side, and bottom of the quilt. The four-patch diamond strip is in the lower right corner of the quilt (see the assembly diagram). Lastly, arrange the edging triangles all around the quilt center.

Using the seam allowance marked on the templates, sew the blocks, diamond strips, and edging triangles together as shown on the assembly diagram. The blocks are sewn together in diagonal rows. Follow the order of assembly carefully to avoid any inset seams. Leave the corner edge triangles until last. Begin by sewing together the diagonal rows at the top left of the quilt (A, B, C, D). Then set this aside and begin again at the lower right corner of the quilt, following the numbers this time. When you have completed 19, sew on the first section (A, B, C, D) as indicated by the number 20. Lastly, sew on the four corner patches (21, 22, 23, 24).

FINISHING QUILT

Press the quilt top. Layer the quilt top, batting, and backing, then baste the layers together (see page 181).

Using light-medium gray thread, stitch-in-the-ditch around the patches. Then machine-quilt two parallel lines through the center of the light and medium patches, following the diamond shape. Machine-quilt squiggles inside the dark diamonds and the edging triangles.

Trim the quilt edges. Then cut the binding fabric on the bias and sew it on around the edge of the quilt (see page 181).

Beautifully weathered gothic masonry provides a good background for St. Marks. Isn't it amazing how the three–dimensional quality of the diamond grid is created by the strangest prints?

BORDERED DIAMONDS

Although the border strips on this quilt are either lighter or darker than the diamonds inside them, the contrast of lightness and darkness is not very great. Likewise, there are alternate rows of lighter diamonds and darker diamonds, but the feel of richness is achieved by keeping the tones fairly close together.

FINISHED SIZE
55 1/2" × 80" (141 cm × 203 cm)

MATERIALS
Use quilting cottons 44–45" (112–114 cm) wide

PATCHWORK FABRICS

Fabric A (diamond lights): 1/2 yd (46 cm) each of at least eight different light-toned and light-medium-toned large-scale floral prints in fuchsias, magentas, reds, golds, corals, pinks, and turquoises; a total of approximately 4 yd (3.7 m)—OR 1/2 yd (46 cm) each of the nine following Rowan fabrics:

Asian Circles in Green; *Big Blooms* in Red and Turquoise; *Cabbage Patch* in Red and Yellow; *Grandiose* in Ochre; *Lake Blossoms* in Taupe; *Lilac Rose* in Lilac; and *Turkish Delight* in Gold

Fabric B (diamond darks): 1/2 yd (46 cm) each of at least eight different dark-medium-toned and light-dark-toned large-scale floral prints in purples, turquoises, reds, and magentas; a total of approximately 4 yd (3.7 m)—OR 1/2 yd (46 cm) each of the eight following Rowan fabrics:

Asian Circles in Dark; *Big Blooms* in Red; *Cabbage Patch* in Red and Magenta; *Lake Blossoms* in Black, Red, and Blue; and *Luscious* in Red

Fabric C (border lights): 1/4 yd (25 cm) each of at least seven different pale-toned and light-toned small-scale and medium-scale florals, polka dots, and circular motif prints in corals, turquoises, pinks, oranges, and gold; a total of approximately 1 3/4 yd (1.6 m)—OR 1/4 yd (25 cm) each of the eight following Rowan fabrics:

Aboriginal Dots in Blue and Rose; *Begonia Leaf* in Gold; *Ivy* in Ochre; *Millefiore* in Orange; *Persimmon* in Orange; and *Spot* in Ice and Turquoise

Fabric D (border darks): 1/4 yd (25 cm) each of at least seven different light-dark-toned and dark-toned small-scale and medium-scale florals and circular motif prints in reds, purple, gray, teal, and moss greens; a total of approximately 1 3/4 yd (1.6 m)—OR 1/4 yd (25 cm) each of the seven following Rowan fabrics:

Aboriginal Dots in Chocolate and Red; *Anemone* in Purple; *Begonia Leaf* in Maroon; *Ivy* in Magenta and Teal; and *Millefiore* in Brown

OTHER INGREDIENTS

Backing fabric: 5 yd (4.6 m) of desired fabric

Binding fabric: 3/4 yd (70 cm) extra of one of the fabric-D prints

Cotton batting: 63" × 87" (155 cm × 220 cm)

Quilting thread: Medium dusky rose thread

Templates: Use template Z (see page 188)

CUTTING PATCHES

Fussy-cut the large diamond patches from the large-scale prints so that there is an attractive display of the motifs in each patch. There is no need to position a single motif in the exact center of the diamond; in fact, the quilt will be more lively if the flowers and leaves are slightly off center. If the fabric design is upright, ignore the grain-line marker (the arrow) on the diamond template and position the diamond upright on the fabric. For nondirectional patterns, follow the grain-line marker.

Be sure to cut the border strips from selvage to selvage so that each strip is long enough to surround one diamond patch.

DIAMOND PATCHES

30 fabric-A diamonds (lights): Fussy-cut 30 template-Z diamonds from fabric A.

30 fabric-B diamonds (darks): Fussy-cut 30 template-Z diamonds from fabric B.

Diamond Block

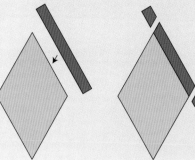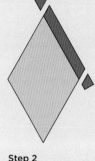

Step 1
Stitch on first strip.

Step 2
Press and trim.

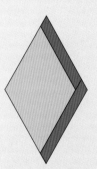

Step 3
Stitch on second strip, press, and trim.

Step 4
Stitch on third strip, press, and trim.

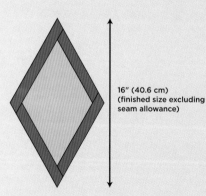

16" (40.6 cm)
(finished size excluding seam allowance)

Step 5
Stitch on fourth strip, press, and trim.

BORDER STRIPS

30 fabric-C strips (lights): Cut 30 strips 1 1/2" (3.8 cm) wide from fabric C, cutting from selvage to selvage and taking four or five strips from each fabric C.

30 fabric-D strips (darks): Cut 30 strips 1 1/2" (3.8 cm) wide from fabric D, cutting from selvage to selvage and taking four or five strips from each fabric D.

MAKING BLOCKS

Sew the borders onto the large diamonds using the seam allowance marked on the template.

60 diamond blocks: Use one fabric-D (dark) strip for the border on each of the 30 fabric-A (light) diamond patches, and one fabric-C strip for the border on each of the 30 fabric-B (dark) diamonds. Follow the block diagram to make each bordered diamond. First, with the right sides facing, align the edge of the strip with the edge of the upper right side of the diamond and sew it in place. Press the border back and trim off the ends of the strip so that it continues the shape of the diamond. Next sew the strip to the bottom right side in the same way, press, and trim. Continue clockwise around the diamond, sewing a border onto the third, then fourth side.

ASSEMBLING TOP

Arrange the blocks as shown on the assembly diagram (page 119), either laying them out on the floor or sticking them to a cotton-flannel design wall. Begin by arranging the 30 light diamonds and 20 dark diamonds, leaving the partial diamonds around the edges till last. There are five horizontal rows of six light diamonds and four horizontal rows of five dark diamonds in between these.

Next return to the remaining 10 dark diamonds, and press them well before cutting them into the partial diamonds needed around the edges. Cut one of these diamonds into quarters to make the four corners of the quilt; cut five horizontally across the center to make the 10 half diamonds needed at the top and bottom of the quilt; and cut the remaining four in half vertically to make the eight half-diamonds needed at the sides of the quilt.

Arrange the partial diamonds randomly around the center of the quilt.

Using the seam allowance marked on the template, sew together the whole bordered diamonds and the partial bordered diamonds in diagonal rows as shown on the assembly diagram.

FINISHING QUILT

Because there is no outside border to stabilize any bias edges on the outside edge of this top, it is a good idea to machine topstitch 1/8" (3 mm) in from the outside edge all around the patchwork. When sewing on the final binding, this staystitching will keep the edge straight.

Bordered Diamonds Assembly

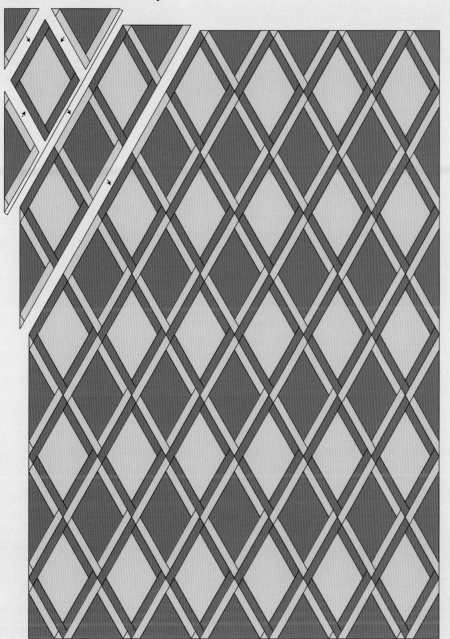

Two different cultures come together in these pictures—the great tiled dome of a Persian mosque mixes with an elegantly knitted cap from Peru. I love the boldness of the diamond grid on the mosque, but the intricate knitting on the multi-diamond hat steals my heart with its array of fine, colored yarns.

KEY

☐ Fabrics A and C

◼ Fabrics B and D

Press the quilt top. Layer the quilt top, batting, and backing, then baste the layers together (see page 181).

Using medium dusky rose thread, stitch-in-the-ditch around the borders and machine-quilt outlines around the flowers in the diamond centers.

Trim the quilt edges. Then cut the binding fabric on the bias and sew it on around the edge of the quilt (see page 181).

NOT-SO-LONE STAR

Each row of diamonds in the big star of this quilt is made with the same fabric. If you are using your own choice of fabrics rather than the ones shown, cut and arrange the patches for a single point of the star to test your colors. Then stand back at a distance from the arrangement to make sure there is enough (but not too much) contrast from row to row.

FINISHED SIZE
98" × 98" (249 cm × 249 cm)

MATERIALS
Use quilting cotton 44–45" (112–114 cm) wide

STAR-PATCH FABRICS

An assortment of 20 different light-toned, medium-toned, and dark-toned prints (17 large-scale florals and three irregular stripes) in predominantly limes, pinks, sky blues, aquas, old gold, and browns, with magenta accents—OR the following 20 Kaffe Fassett fabrics:

Fabric A: 1/4 yd (25 cm) of *Kimono* in Crimson

Fabric B: 3/4 yd (70 cm) of *Guinea Flower* in Pink

Fabric C: 3/4 yd (70 cm) of *Zinnia* in Aqua

Fabric D: 3/4 yd (70 cm) of *Big Blooms* in Turquoise

Fabric E: 1/2 yd (46 cm) of *Asian Circles* in Ochre

Fabric F: 1/2 yd (46 cm) of *Diagonal Stripes* in Ochre

Fabric G: 3/4 yd (70 cm) of *Star Flowers* in Duck Egg

Fabric H: 3/4 yd (70 cm) of *Clouds* in Magenta

Fabric J: 1 yd (92 cm) of *Big Blooms* in Pink

Fabric K: 1 yd (92 cm) of *Big Blooms* in Duck Egg

Fabric L: 3/4 yd (70 cm) of *Clouds* in Ochre

Fabric M: 1/2 yd (46 cm) of *Asian Circles* in Green

Fabric N: 1/4 yd (25 cm) of *Diagonal Stripes* in Pink

Fabric O: 1/4 yd (25 cm) of *Dahlia Blooms* in Spring

Fabric P: 1/8 yd (13 cm) of *Floating Flowers* in Green

Fabric Q: 1/8 yd (13 cm) of *Dahlia Blooms* in Fig

Fabric R: 1/8 yd (13 cm) of *Millefiore* in Green

Fabric S: 1/8 yd (13 cm) of *Diagonal Stripes* in Yellow

Fabric T: 1/8 yd (13 cm) of *Zinnia* in Pink

Fabric U: 1/4 yd (25 cm) of *Clouds* in Duck Egg

BACKGROUND-PATCH FABRIC

Fabric V: 5 yd (4.6 m) of a medium-toned large-scale floral print in oranges, rust, and magenta pinks on a maroon ground—OR Kaffe Fassett *Lake Blossoms* in Red

OTHER INGREDIENTS

Backing fabric: 9 yd (8.3 m) of desired fabric

Binding fabric: 1 yd (92 cm) extra of fabric V

Cotton batting: 105" × 105" (265 cm × 265 cm)

Quilting thread: Coral-colored thread

Templates: Use templates M, N, and O (see page 189)

SPECIAL FABRIC NOTE

The Kaffe Fassett fabrics listed for the quilt are the ones used for the quilt pictured. If you are using these fabrics, you might like to substitute *Zinnia* in Pink for the *Big Blooms* in Pink in row 9 of the big star—this is the improvement I would like to make on my next version of this quilt to give more contrast in color between the diamonds in rows 9 and 10. Keep this in mind if you are using your own choice of fabrics: Make sure there is just enough contrast in color or tone between the rows of diamonds in the stars. The dark-toned colors should be smoky and the lights high and fresh.

With this quilt, I wanted to both meld patterns and colors as well as create dramatic breaks in flow. I started with a very strong background, my magenta and wine Lake Blossoms print. Then I chose stripes, big florals, and dotty prints for the bursts of energy that are the stars. If you're using scraps to form your stars, try them out before stitching. Mocking up the combination on your work wall doesn't cost you anything but a little time and fabric, and it so often brings a much higher level of success than just blindly sewing away.

CUTTING PATCHES

Cut the diamond patches for the big star first so that you can use the leftovers for the small stars in the corners of the quilt if you wish.

BIG STAR

The big star is made up of eight points that are sewn together in blocks. Cut enough matching diamonds for all 17 rows in all eight blocks as instructed. Be sure to use a different grain line on the diamond template for the odd-numbered and even-numbered rows of diamonds; this will ensure that bias edges will be matched to straight-grain edges to stabilize the joined patches. Keep the diamonds in marked piles for easy assembly of the blocks and so that the grain lines do not become mixed up.

Row 1—8 diamonds: From fabric A, cut one template-M diamond for each of the eight blocks—for a total of 8 diamonds.

Row 2—16 diamonds: From fabric B, cut two template-M diamonds for each of the eight blocks—for a total of 16 diamonds.

Row 3—24 diamonds: From fabric C, cut three template-M diamonds for each of the eight blocks—for a total of 24 diamonds.

Row 4—32 diamonds: From fabric D, cut four template-M diamonds for each of the eight blocks—for a total of 32 diamonds.

Row 5—40 diamonds: From fabric E, cut five template-M diamonds for each of the eight blocks—for a total of 40 diamonds.

Row 6—48 diamonds: From fabric F, cut six template-M diamonds for each of the eight blocks—for a total of 48 diamonds.

Row 7—56 diamonds: From fabric G, cut seven template-M diamonds for each of the eight blocks—for a total of 56 diamonds.

Row 8—64 diamonds: From fabric H, cut eight template-M diamonds for each of the eight blocks—for a total of 64 diamonds.

Row 9—72 diamonds: From fabric J, cut nine template-M diamonds for each of the eight blocks—for a total of 72 diamonds.

Row 10—64 diamonds: From fabric K, cut eight template-M diamonds for each of the eight blocks—for a total of 64 diamonds.

Row 11—56 diamonds: From fabric B, cut seven template-M diamonds for each of the eight blocks—for a total of 56 diamonds.

Row 12—48 diamonds: From fabric L, cut six template-M diamonds for each of the eight blocks—for a total of 48 diamonds.

Row 13—40 diamonds: From fabric M, cut five template-M diamonds for each of the eight blocks—for a total of 40 diamonds.

Row 14—32 diamonds: From fabric C, cut four template-M diamonds for each of the eight blocks—for a total of 32 diamonds.

Row 15—24 diamonds: From fabric D, cut three template-M diamonds for each of the eight blocks—for a total of 24 diamonds.

Row 16—16 diamonds: From fabric N, cut two template-M diamonds for each of the eight blocks—for a total of 16 diamonds.

Row 17—8 diamonds: From fabric O, cut one template-M diamonds for each of the eight blocks—for a total of 8 diamonds.

SMALL CORNER STARS

The four small stars, one at each corner, are also made up of eight points that are sewn together in small blocks. Cut these diamonds for these stars separately since each star is different. Be sure to use a different grain line on the diamond template for the odd-numbered and even-numbered rows of diamonds as you did for the big star.

First small star: For row 1 (row at the center of the star), cut eight template-M diamonds from fabric H; for row 2, cut 16 template-M diamonds from fabric J; and for row 3 (the star tips), cut eight template-M diamonds from fabric T.

Second small star: For row 1, cut eight template-M diamonds from fabric U; for row 2, cut eight template-M diamonds from fabric P and eight from fabric L; and for row 3, cut eight template-M diamonds from fabric K.

Third small star: For row 1, cut eight template-M diamonds from fabric D; for row 2, cut eight template-M diamonds from fabric S and eight from fabric U; and for row 3, cut eight template-M diamonds from fabric M.

Fourth small star: For row 1, cut eight template-M diamonds from fabric Q; for row 2, cut 16 template-M diamonds from fabric R; and for row 3, cut eight template-M diamonds from fabric O.

BACKGROUND FOR SMALL-STAR BLOCKS

When cutting the patches for the background from the large-scale floral (and when arranging the background pieces), do not attempt to match the fabric motifs or cut them so that the fabric will all face in one direction when sewn in place; the background will look better if the motifs face in various directions.

16 template-N squares: From fabric V, cut four template-N squares for each of the four small-star blocks—for a total of 16 squares.

32 template-O triangles: From fabric V, cut eight template-O triangles for each of the four small-star blocks—for a total of 32 triangles.

8 short border strips: From fabric V, cut two border strips 4" × 22 1/4" (10.2 cm × 56.5 cm) for each of the four small-star blocks—for a total of 8 short strips.

8 long border strips: From fabric V, cut two border strips 4" × 29 1/4" (10.2 cm × 74.3 cm) for each of the four small-star blocks—for a total of 8 short strips.

BACKGROUND FOR BIG STAR

The background for the big star is filled in at each of the four corners with the small-star blocks. The remainder of the background is filled in with eight large triangle patches. Make your own template for these triangles. Draw a right-angled triangle measuring 20 1/4" (51.4 cm) along the two matching sides of the triangle and 28 11/16" (72.9 cm) along the long diagonal of the triangle. Then

Big-Star Block

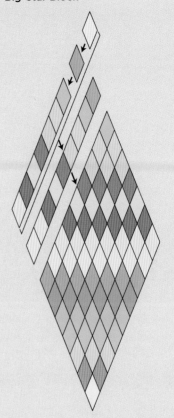

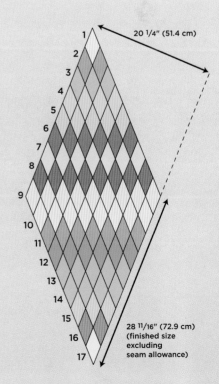

20 1/4" (51.4 cm)

28 11/16" (72.9 cm) (finished size excluding seam allowance)

Small-Star Block

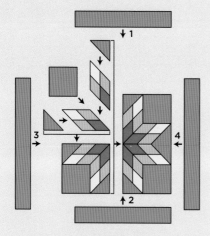

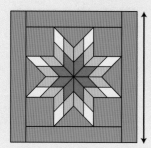

28 ^{11/16}" (72.9 cm) square (finished size excluding seam allowance)

add a 1/4" (6 mm) seam allowance all around the edge of the template. Use this template to cut the eight large triangles from fabric V.

MAKING BLOCKS

Make the blocks using the seam allowance marked on the templates.

8 big-star blocks: Using the patches cut for each of the eight big-star blocks, arrange the diamonds in 17 rows as shown on the Big-Star Block diagram (page 123). Once each of the diagonal rows is sewn together, sew the diagonal rows to each other as shown.

4 small-star blocks: Using the patches cut for each of the small stars, plus the patches cut for the small-star background, sew the pieces together as shown on the Small-Star Block diagram.

ASSEMBLING TOP

Arrange the blocks and big triangle patches as shown on the assembly diagram (page 125), either laying them out on the floor or sticking them to a cotton-flannel design wall.

Using the seam allowance marked on the templates throughout, sew together two of the big-star blocks, matching diamond rows 1–9 as shown in the assembly diagram. Then sew one of the small-star blocks in place between these two big-star blocks and a large background triangle to each big-star block. Sew together each of the remaining four quarters of the quilt in the same way. Then sew the quarters together in pairs. Lastly, sew the two halves of the quilt top together.

FINISHING QUILT

Press the quilt top. Layer the quilt top, batting, and backing, then baste the layers together (see page 181).

Using coral-colored thread, machine-quilt wavy convex curves from corner to corner of each diamond patch so that the stitching is about 1/4" (6 mm) from the outer edge of the diamond at its widest distance from the edge. Machine-quilt meandering lines all over the background.

Trim the quilt edges. Then cut the binding fabric on the bias and sew it on around the edge of the quilt (see page 181).

Not-So-Lone Star Assembly

KEY

☐ Fabric A	☐ Fabric D	☐ Fabric G
☐ Fabric B	☐ Fabric E	☐ Fabric H
☐ Fabric C	☐ Fabric F	☐ Fabric J

☐ Fabric K	☐ Fabric N	☐ Fabric Q	☐ Fabric T
☐ Fabric L	☐ Fabric O	☐ Fabric R	☐ Fabric U
☐ Fabric M	☐ Fabric P	☐ Fabric S	☐ Fabric V

QUARTER CIRCLES

For me, the quarter circle is the most difficult shape to find in the world around us, but it is there—quarters of cheese, round fruits cut into quarters, circular windows divided into quarters. Drivers in England are presented with quarter circles nearly every day when they pass the sign indicating the end of speed restrictions: a red and blue circle with a cross overlaid upon it. The quarter circle is also a favorite of paving mosaickers and bricklayers. I also think of the graphic black-and-white stone pavements in Portugal that give such rhythm and visual movement to sidewalks.

In the formal topiary of French gardens, we find box hedges cut in great geometric forms often with quarter circles. In a million flywheels painted varying colors on pipe systems around the world we see this shape in four segments. I, for one, am always delighted to find neat stacks of cut wood in Switzerland and Scandinavian countries creating primitive quarter circles. But my all-time favorite example of the quarter circle is within the glorious iron lacework on Victorian porches in New Zealand and Australia. Often this ironwork is painted the typical black, but I was once dazzled by a deep pink example, which is shown on the previous page (bottom left). What a celebration for the eye it is! The pink leaves of the hedge draw out the intense pink of the ironwork.

Searching for more quarter circles to seduce your eye, I discovered a merry-go-round in London painted in slightly off primary colors (see page 126, top center). A pared-down functional design, it makes an un-assuming but sharp statement, with the plain colors self-confidently filling the gutsy shapes. Always keep your eyes open for geometry or you'll miss things like this that seem mundane at first glance.

Less colorful but with great geometry are the cast-iron protectors I spied around the bases of trees on a nearby street. I am a pattern junky, so not only colorful pattern gets me going. The geometry of pattern in neutral shades catches my eye just as easily; it can create a melody of its own. That's why manhole covers are to me the poetry of the street.

In quilting the quarter circle is a surprisingly zesty shape, adding a fresh approach to circles by breaking them into angular forms. The traditional jockey cap block, which is composed of four quarter circles in contrasting colors combined into a circle, makes a very cheeky presentation. Hearts and gizzards, which utilizes quarter circles in highly contrasting colors like red and white, is another of my favorites.

One of the most exciting motifs that uses a base of quarter circles is the fan shape. I used it in Tumbling Fans (page 131), inspired by an old quilt motif I found in a book called *Quilts of Illusion* by Laura Fisher. The fans in Fisher's book sat on dimensional box shapes like elongated tumbling blocks, and that is how I designed my version. But a friend of mine, Judy Baldwin, got the idea from one of her books to sew four of the fans together to create a sunburst that is really powerful. Because Judy used husky contrasting solids, her quilt really makes a dramatic statement. Check out the photo of it on the opposite page.

Fans in the shape of quarter circles are also quite common in corners of very ornate crazy quilts and give the eye a place to rest within all of that random detail. Another classic use of this form is the overlapping scallop shape, or fan shell, that I'm sure was inspired by that same effect in old Roman mosaics.

Judy Baldwin's version of Tumbling Fans with its autumnal contrasts sits handsomely next to the sharp black-and-white Elizabethan house timbers (opposite page). Softer half circles appear in an old garden wall in London and on a Portuguese square, dancing with overlapped scallops (above).

◀ DAMASK QUARTERS

On one of my trips to visit Liza in Pennsylvania, I found her working on a jockey cap made of beautiful fresco-colored damasks. She loved the colors but wasn't certain they were jiving in this pattern, so I started playing and came up with the simple layout you see here. The unrelieved repetition creates a strong vibration for me, especially in these muted colors. I particularly like the taupes, pinky and lavender grays, and khaki tones; they give a wonderfully husky base to the brighter limes, sulfur yellows, and terra-cottas. We used Fan Flowers, a print from a few collections back, in the border and were surprised by the way it echoes the quarter-circle shapes. Liza chose ocher Paper Fans (one of our ongoing classics) for the backing, which is perfection to my eye.

See instructions on pages 134–137.

▶ TUMBLING FANS

An old pattern that grabbed me every time I came across it, the powerful tumbling fans begged to be interpreted in my darker fabrics; the result reminds me of the stained-glass windows in American houses built in the 1920s. I kept all the quarter-circle fan bases the same dark tone to emphasize their shape but would love to see this in bright circus colors or in all the neutral tones of a stony beach. Alternatively, pearly grays would be elegant and make this layout look like an ancient stone mosaic. Since the geometry of Tumbling Fans is quite like a motif found in marquetry, it would also be good to see this in honey browns, with the wide range of color variation found in that woody world.

See instructions on pages 138–143.

BOW-TIE CIRCLES

Here's another classic old layout for the versatile bow tie. I like the way the ties in many shades of red create a strong grid through which we see quarter circles in the background made up of pinks, lavenders, and mint green, and then how the two palettes are switched at the border: The red becomes the background and the ligher colors are used for the ties. We worked two full rows of bow ties at the border, but one row of them might create a more pleasing proportion. I enjoyed shooting this graphic quilt on this strong, fading pink bridge. I only wish we could have stopped London traffic long enough to shoot it from the middle of the road.

See instructions on pages 144-147.

DAMASK QUARTERS

Piecing these blocks requires an intermediate level of sewing skill, but once you stitch a few curves they do become easier. We chose beautiful hand-dyed damasks for the blocks, but a similar effect can be achieved with the solid Kaffe Fassett fabrics called *Shot Cotton*. You could also try tea-dyeing some fabrics to create the right colors.

FINISHED SIZE

62" × 80" (157.5 cm × 203 cm)

MATERIALS

Use quilting cottons 44–45" (112–114 cm) wide

PATCHWORK FABRICS

Fabric A (darks): 1/2 yd (46 cm) each of at least eight different mostly dark-toned (and a couple medium-toned) solid fabrics in a tea-dyed effect palette of olive greens, mink browns, gray-lavenders, and plum; a total of approximately 4 yd (3.7 m)

Fabric B (lights): 1/4–1/2 yd (25–46 cm) each of at least eight different mostly pale-toned and light-toned (and a few medium-toned) solid fabrics in a tea-dyed effect palette of steel blue, soft lime greens, terra-cottas, dusky rose, gold, and taupe; a total of approximately 3 yd (2.8 m)

Fabric C (inner-border fabric): 1 3/4 yd (1.6 m) of a large-scale floral print in medium caramel with coral highlights—OR Kaffe Fassett *Fan Flowers* in Gold

Fabric D (outer-border fabric): 2 1/8 yd (2 m) of a large-scale stylized floral print in dark caramel—OR Kaffe Fassett *Potentilla* in Gold

OTHER INGREDIENTS

Backing fabric: 4 yd (3.7 m) of desired fabric

Binding fabric: 3/4 yd (70 cm) of a dark brown fabric

Cotton batting: 69" × 87" (175 cm × 220 cm)

Quilting thread: Gold-colored thread

Templates: Use templates K and L (see page 186)

CUTTING PATCHES

Most of the background shapes on the blocks in the quilt center are cut from fabric B (the lighter fabrics) and most of the fan shapes are cut from fabric A (the darker fabrics), but the "twinkling" appearance of the quilt comes from the reversal of the light and dark areas on a portion of the blocks.

QUILT CENTER

280 background shapes: Cut 250 template-K background shapes mostly from fabric A (darks), and about 30 from fabric B (lights)—for a total of 280 background shapes.

280 fan shapes: Cut about 250 template-L fan shapes from fabric B (lights), and about 30 from fabric A (darks)—for a total of 280 fan shapes.

BORDERS

If you are using a stylized floral fabric that has a directional print (like the suggested Kaffe Fassett fabric) for the inner border, match the pattern at the seams, piecing strips together as required.

4 inner-border strips: From fabric C, cut two strips 6 1/2" × 60 1/2" (16.5 cm × 153.7 cm) for the side borders; then cut two strips 6 1/2" × 54 1/2" (16.5 cm × 138.5 cm) for the top and bottom borders.

4 outer-border strips: From fabric D, cut two strips 4 1/2" × 72 1/2" (11.5 cm × 184.2 cm) for the side borders; then cut two strips 4 1/2" × 62 1/2" (11.5 cm × 159 cm) for the top and bottom borders.

The scallop is probably the most often used of the partial-circle motifs. Here it is in jewel-tone blues as a floor treatment (above top). Isn't it perky the way this little quarter circle starts at the base of the decorative fans in this cushion I designed in the old-fashioned crazy-quilt style (above)?

MAKING BLOCKS

Make the blocks using the seam allowance marked on the templates.

280 blocks: For each of the 280 blocks, select one background shape and one fan shape. For most of the blocks, select a fan shape that is lighter than the background shape. But for 30 to 40 blocks, select a fan shape that is darker than the background shape.

Make each block as shown in the block diagram, sewing the fan shape and the background shape together along the curved edge. To make stitching easier, clip the concave edge of the background shape before pinning the pieces together. Pin at each end of the fan shape and once at the center. Ease the edges of the pieces together as you machine-stitch the seam. If you find this difficult to do, then baste the pieces together before machine-stitching.

Damask Quarters Block

3" (7.6 cm) square
(finished size excluding
seam allowance)

ASSEMBLING TOP

Arrange the blocks as shown on the assembly diagram (page 137), either laying them out on the floor or sticking them to a cotton-flannel design wall. There are 14 blocks across the quilt and 20 blocks from top to bottom. Make sure the colors are well mixed.

Using the seam allowance marked on the templates, sew the blocks together in 20 rows of 14 blocks. Then sew the rows together.

Using the seam allowance marked on the templates for the border seams, sew the long inner-border strips to the sides of the quilt center and the short inner-border strips to the top and bottom of the quilt center.

Next sew the long outer-border strips to the sides of the quilt and the short outer-border strips to the top and bottom of the quilt.

FINISHING QUILT

Press the quilt top. Layer the quilt top, batting, and backing, then baste the layers together (see page 181).

Using gold-colored thread, stitch-in-the-ditch around the outer edge of each of the blocks in the quilt center and free-motion machine-quilt around the flowers in the borders.

Trim the quilt edges. Then cut the binding fabric on the bias and sew it on around the edge of the quilt (see page 181).

Damask Quarters Assembly

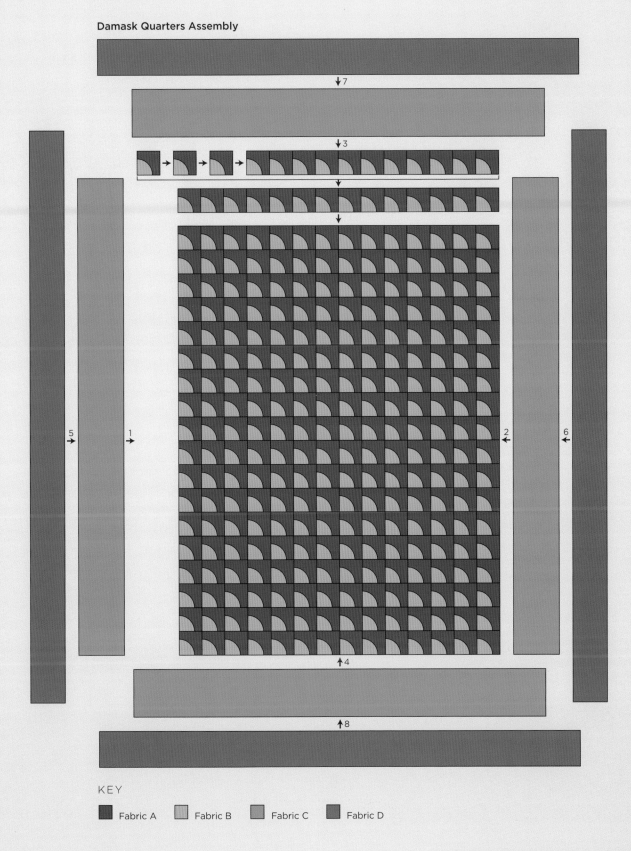

KEY

■ Fabric A   ■ Fabric B   ■ Fabric C   ■ Fabric D

TUMBLING FANS

Making this quilt is much easier than it looks. The patches of the fans are sewn together directly onto paper templates using the easy-to-master paper foundation piecing technique—the paper is simply torn away behind the patches once the quilt center is completely assembled. The dark quarter circles are hand-stitched to the bases of the fans.

FINISHED SIZE
72 1/2" × 79 3/4" (184 cm × 202.5 cm)

MATERIALS
Use quilting cottons 44–45" (112–114 cm) wide

PATCHWORK FABRICS

Fabric A (light fan patches): 1/4 yd (25 cm) each of at least eight different light-toned and medium-toned solids and small-scale prints in aquas, turquoises, lavender, lime, ocher, and light rust; a total of approximately 2 yd (1.9 m)

Fabric B (dark fan patches): 1/4 yd (25 cm) each of at least eight different dark-medium-toned and dark-toned solids and small-scale prints in rusts, purple, maroon, cobalt blue, scarlet, and teal; a total of approximately 2 yd (1.9 m)

Fabric C (light tumbling-block patches): 1/4 yd (25 cm) each of at least 12 different light-toned and medium-toned solids, small-scale prints, and stripes in a smoky palette of taupes, khaki, olives, leaf green, and gunmetal lavenders; a total of approximately 3 yd (2.8 m)

Fabric D (dark tumbling-block patches): 1/4 yd (25 cm) each of at least 12 different dark-toned solids, small-scale prints, and stripes in mulled wine, purples, bottle greens, charcoal, and burgundy; a total of approximately 3 yd (2.8 m)

Fabric E (quarter-circle fan bases): 1/2 yd (46 cm) of a solid in black—OR Kaffe Fassett *Shot Cotton* in Coal

Fabric F (borders): 2 1/4 yd (2.1 m) of a large-scale paisley print in greens, orange, and purple on a black ground—OR Kaffe Fassett *Paisley Jungle* in Moss

Fabric G (border corners): 1/2 yd (46 cm) of a print with large circular motifs in medium-toned bright colors on a black ground—OR Kaffe Fassett *Turkish Delight* in Jewel

OTHER INGREDIENTS

Backing fabric: 5 yd (4.6 m) of desired fabric

Binding fabric: 3/4 yd (70 cm) of a purple polka dot on a black ground

Cotton batting: 80" × 88" (200 cm × 220 cm)

Quilting thread: Medium taupe thread

Templates: Use templates M, M reverse, N, and O (see page 182)

SPECIAL FABRIC NOTE

Many Kaffe Fassett *Shot Cotton* solid fabrics were used for the fans and tumbling blocks in this quilt. If you would like to add them to your selection for fabrics A, B, C, and D, buy them and take them along when choosing the prints and stripes to add to the mix. Here is a list of the ones to purchase:

Shot Cotton in Clay, Terracotta, Brick, Prune, Pewter, Pine, Sludge, Nut, Slate, Moss, Cassis, Sage, Bordeaux, Veridian, Ginger, Bittersweet, Aegean, Jade, Lime, Mustard, Opal, Persimmon, Scarlet, Forget-Me-Not, Caramel, Moor, and Chartreuse.

Put aside the brightest colors for the fans (fabrics A and B) and separate the duller ones into a light and dark group (fabrics C and D) for the tumbling-block patches.

CUTTING PATCHES

Cut all the patches for the quilt, except those for the fans, which are made with the paper foundation piecing method.

242 tumbling-block patches: From fabric C (lights), cut 121 template-O parallelograms; and from fabric D (darks), cut 121 template-O-reverse parallelograms—for a total of 242 tumbling-block patches.

115 quarter-circle fan bases: Make a cardboard appliqué template from template N (see page 182). Using the cardboard template, trace 115 template-N shapes onto fabric E, leaving space around each piece for the 1/4" (6 mm) seam allowance. Cut out each shape 1/4" (6 mm) outside the outline.

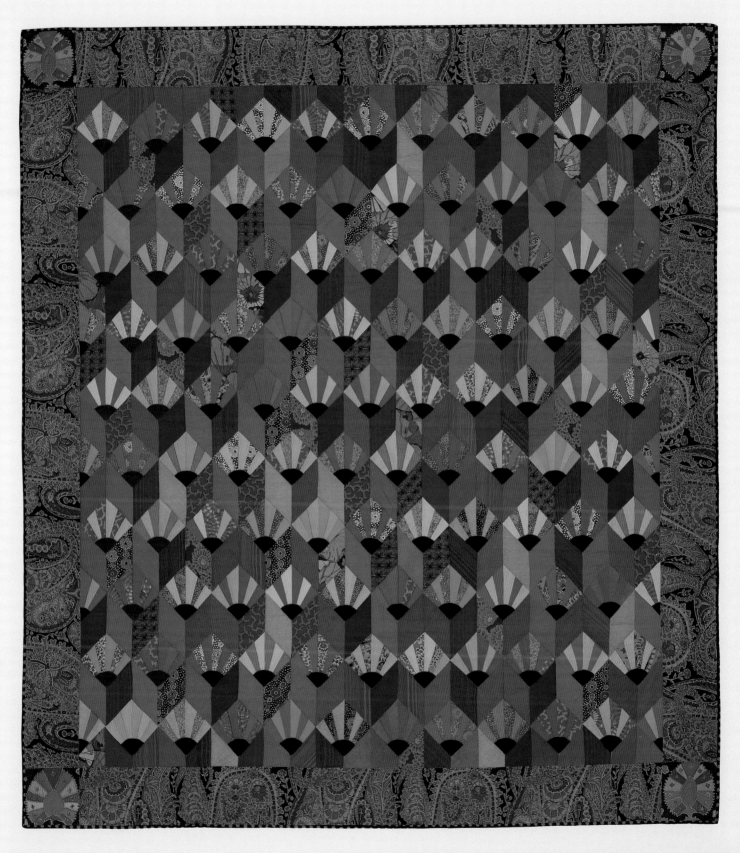

Yet another example of scallops in mosaic (above top). The bright centers and ombré shading lift the design. Contrast that soft shading with the bold excitement of Judy Baldwin's Tumbling Fans variation where the fans join together to form Japanese rising sun flags (above). The autumn-toned palette of solids adds to the boldness of the impact. You could do Tumbling Fans in the tones of the mosaic for a more subtle faded effect that would be just as beautiful. The design is strong enough to shine through a quieter palette.

4 border strips: From fabric F, cut two strips 6 1/2" × 68 1/4" (16.5 cm × 173.4 cm) for the side borders; then cut two strips 6 1/2" × 61" (16.5 cm × 155 cm) for the top and bottom borders. Center the print pattern within these border strips, matching the opposite sides as closely as possible to each other.

4 border corner squares: From fabric G, fussy-cut four squares 6 1/2" × 6 1/2" (16.5 cm × 16.5 cm), centering a large motif within each square.

MAKING FOUNDATION-PIECED FANS

The fan patches are sewn together with the easy paper foundation piecing technique. For this, each fan requires a paper foundation for each half of the fan. Make 110 photocopies of template M and 110 photocopies of template M reverse (see page 182). (Do not photocopy a photocopy because this can distort the very accurate size of the design.) Cut out each paper foundation exactly around the outer line (there is no seam allowance on this paper foundation).

PREPARING PATCHES

To begin the first half-fan block, first choose a fabric A (a light-toned fabric) and a fabric B (a dark-toned fabric) for the patches. Take a template-M paper foundation and roughly cut a fabric piece for each numbered area of the foundation, alternating the two colors; allow at least 1/2" (12 mm) extra fabric all around the edge of the patch area on the paper foundation. There is no need to pay attention to the fabric grain line when cutting and stitching the patches, because the paper foundation they are being stitched onto will provide the necessary stability.

STITCHING FIRST HALF-FAN BLOCK

Stitch the patches to the paper foundation as explained for the first rim block for the Bicycle Wheel quilt on page 176, but begin the seam slightly beyond the paper and end it inside the triangle as marked on the template. Sew the seam between section no. 1 and section no. 2 almost to the point, and the seam between section no. 2 and section no. 3 only three-quarters of the way to the point—these seam lengths don't have to be exact because they will eventually be covered by the fan base appliqué. If you were to sew the seams all the way to the point, the patches would become too lumpy in this area.

FINISHING FIRST HALF-FAN BLOCK

Once the three patches have been stitched in place and pressed, trim the fabric all around the half-fan block 1/4" (6 mm) from the paper—this extra 1/4" (6 mm) is the seam allowance that will be taken up when the quilt top is assembled. Do not remove the paper yet.

MAKING REMAINING HALF-FAN BLOCKS

Following the instructions for the first half-fan block, make a template-M-reverse half-fan block to match the first half of the fan, positioning the colors so that they will alternate across the fan when the fan is stitched together.

Tumbling Fans Assembly

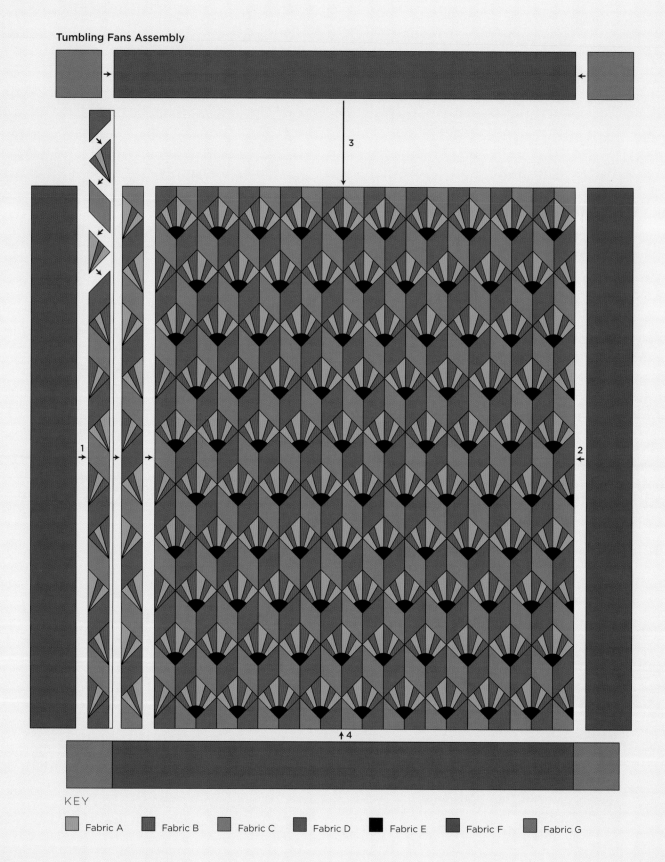

KEY

Fabric A   Fabric B   Fabric C   Fabric D   Fabric E   Fabric F   Fabric G

Make a total of 110 matching pairs of template-M and template-M-reverse half-fan blocks in the same way. Do not remove the papers.

ASSEMBLING TOP

Arrange the quilt center as shown on the assembly diagram (page 142), either laying out the patches on the floor or sticking them to a cotton-flannel design wall. Start with a horizontal row of 11 fans across the top of the quilt, then add a row of tumbling block patches above and below this row, alternating the dark and light patches and making sure that the vertical sides of the parallelograms are the straight-grain edges. (The top row of tumbling block patches and the bottom row will be trimmed later; the trim line is marked on the template.) Working downward, continue adding horizontal rows of fans and tumbling block patches in the same way. Every other fan row ends and begins with a half fan as shown on the assembly diagram. There are a total of 10 horizontal rows of fans and 11 horizontal rows of tumbling block patches.

Using the seam allowance marked on the templates throughout, sew the blocks together in vertical rows as shown on the assembly diagram, then sew the vertical rows together. Trim the top and bottom of the quilt top to the position marked on template O.

To appliqué the fan base to the first fan, begin by marking the shape of the quarter circle at the base of the fan using the appliqué template (template N). Then gently remove the paper at the back of the fan and stitch the fan base in place, turning under the seam allowance. Sew a fan base to each fan in the same way, trimming the bases along the side edges of the quilt to fit the half fans there. Be sure to sew on all the fan bases before stitching on the borders.

Sew one of the long border strips to each side of the quilt center. Then sew one border square to each end of the two short border strips and stitch these borders to the top and bottom of the quilt.

FINISHING QUILT

Press the quilt top. Layer the quilt top, batting, and backing, then baste the layers together (see page 181).

Using medium taupe thread, stitch-in-the-ditch around each patch in the quilt center. Then outline-quilt around the large motifs in the border and the border corner squares.

Trim the quilt edges. Then cut the binding fabric on the bias and sew it on around the edge of the quilt (see page 181).

This is a scrap of needlepoint I picked up at a flea market and, like many such finds, it has fed me much inspiration. I used this idea on a much enlarged scale to knit a throw and large floor cushion, but I sent my colored inner shading on the diagonal up the lattice, which gives it quite a different feel. This would be a good patchwork idea if it were treated like St. Marks on page 94, with the shading in prints of different intensities.

BOW-TIE CIRCLES

The easy-to-stitch blocks of this quilt are used to form circle shapes instead of bow ties. The fabrics shown are all from the Rowan range, but any small-scale or medium-scale prints will work. For a simpler quilt and to give the center more impact, omit the outer row of blocks on the border.

FINISHED SIZE
96" × 96" (244 cm × 244 cm)

MATERIALS
Use quilting cottons 44–45" (112–114 cm) wide

PATCHWORK FABRICS

Fabric A (darks): 1/2 yd (46 cm) each of at least 15 different medium-toned and dark-toned small-scale and medium-scale prints in corals, purples, magentas, lilacs, and high bright reds; a total of approximately 7 1/2 yd (7 m)—OR 1/2 yd (46 cm) each of the following 15 Rowan fabrics:

Spot in Purple, Magenta, and Red; *Silhouette Rose* in Wine and Rose; *Paperweight* in Paprika; *Aboriginal Dot* in Orange; *Clover* in Red; *Dancing Leaves* in Heather; *Ikat Polka Dot* in Scarlet; *Guinea Flower* in Pink; *Two-Toned Stripe* in Red; *Paper Fans* in Red; *Stencil Carnation* in Rose; and *Asha* in Wine

Fabric B (lights): 1/2 yd (46 cm) each of at least 13 different pale-toned and light-toned small-scale and medium-scale prints in pinks, lavenders, pistachio greens, and mauves; a total of approximately 6 1/2 yd (6 m)—OR 1/2 yd (46 cm) each of the following 13 Rowan fabrics:

Daisy in Pink; *Stencil Carnation* in Lilac and Periwinkle; *Floating Flowers* in Pastel; *Guinea Flower* in Mauve; *Ivy* in Lilac; *Aboriginal Dot* in Pink; *Clover* in Lilac; *Lichen* in Celadon; *Roman Glass* in Pink; *Spot* in Pink and Mint; and *Woven Checks* in Mint

OTHER INGREDIENTS

Backing fabric: 9 yd (8.3 m) of desired fabric

Binding fabric: 3/4 yd (70 cm) extra of one of the fabric-A prints

Cotton batting: 103" × 103" (260 cm × 260 cm)

Quilting thread: Medium pink thread

Templates: Use templates P and Q (see page 184)

CUTTING PATCHES

Cut the patches in sets for each block and keep the sets carefully pinned together.

PATCHES FOR QUILT CENTER

144 center blocks: For each of the 144 center blocks, cut two large template-P squares from the same fabric B, then cut two large template-P squares and two small template-Q squares from the same fabric A.

PATCHES FOR BORDERS

112 border blocks: For each of the 112 border blocks, cut two large template-P squares from the same fabric A, then cut two large template-P squares and two small template-Q squares from the same fabric B.

PREPARING PATCHES

For each of the bow-tie circles blocks, you will need to sew one of the small template-Q squares to one corner of each of the contrasting squares—on the center quilt blocks, the small fabric-A (dark) squares are stitched to the large fabric-B (light) squares; on the border blocks, the small fabric-B (light) squares are stitched to the large fabric-A (dark) squares.

Before stitching on the small squares for each block, use a pencil to draw a diagonal line from corner to corner on the wrong side of each of the two

Sewing on Contrasting Corner

Step 1
Stitch.

Step 2
Trim.

Step 3
Press corner back.

Bow-Tie Circles Block

6" (15 cm) square
(finished size
excluding
seam allowance)

These two mosaic ideas both use square elements to create quarter-circleness. The pavement (above) starts with quarter circles at the center, then boxy shapes expanding outward. The finer mosaic (above top) uses small-cut squares to create endless flower petal shapes.

small squares (this is shown as the stitching line on template Q). Next pin a small square to each of the large squares, with right sides together and with the edges of the fabrics carefully aligned. Stitch each small square in place along the stitching line as shown in step 1 of the diagram. Then trim each seam allowance to 1/4" (6 mm) and press the corners back as shown in steps 2 and 3.

MAKING BLOCKS

Make the blocks using the seam allowance marked on the templates.

QUILT CENTER

144 center blocks: For each of the 144 center blocks, sew together the two fabric-A squares and the two fabric-B squares with the corner patches as shown in the block diagram.

BORDERS

112 border blocks: For each of the 112 border blocks, sew together the two fabric-B squares and the two fabric-A squares with the corner patches in the same way.

ASSEMBLING TOP

Arrange the blocks as shown on the assembly diagram (page 147), either laying them out on the floor or sticking them to a cotton-flannel design wall. For the quilt center, position 12 rows of 12 blocks, alternating the direction of the bow ties to form the circle shapes. Surround the center with two concentric rows of the border blocks, again alternating the direction of the bow ties to form the circles. It is easy to get lost while arranging the blocks, so take your time. The quilt center creates the effect of light balls on a dark background and the border creates the effect of dark balls on a light background.

Using the seam allowance marked on the templates throughout, first sew the blocks for the quilt center together in 12 horizontal rows of 12 blocks, then sew the 12 rows together as shown on the assembly diagram.

For each side border, sew together two vertical rows of 12 blocks, then sew them to the sides of the quilt center. For the top and bottom borders, sew together two horizontal rows of 16 blocks, then sew them in place.

FINISHING QUILT

Press the quilt top. Layer the quilt top, batting, and backing, then baste the layers together (see page 181).

Using medium pink thread, machine-quilt meandering lines over the quilt.

Trim the quilt edges. Then cut the binding fabric on the bias and sew it on around the edge of the quilt (see page 181).

Bow-Tie Circles Assembly

KEY

Fabric A   Fabric B

CIRCLES

The gorgeous warm shape of the circle reminds us that the world is round and the very eyes we view it with are round. Circles are easy to find nearly everywhere. Look up from this page at this very moment and you'll probably see at least one. Take note of architectural details, pipes, barrels, tires, traffic signs, flowerpots, carpet designs, buttons, soda cans, teacups, mirrors, the moon, the sun, and on and on. Here's what I see when I pause from writing: sewing spools, a crocheted hat studded with round buttons, a vase painted with round flowers, the knobs on the chest of drawers in which I store my yarns, and the round, staring eyes of a Balinese mask.

Outside, roughly cut circles in paving stones often delight me. Even old dumps full of tires or rusty barrels light me up. Round shapes, such as domed doors and circular windows, soften the hard edge of the modern cityscape.

When I design my fabric collections, I find myself gravitating toward the circle more than any other shape. Flower heads become large polka dots on one print, and bicycle wheels inspire another. Recently, I did a big paperweight design—small circles on larger ones. Around the same time I designed a knitted fabric that looks like a checkerboard of multicolored squares with a circle filling each square. I call it "Coins in Boxes," but I could have just as easily named it "Eye Shadow" since it reminds me of the eye shadow displays at cosmetic counters.

I was raised in a log house in California with the round logs giving us perfect circles at the corners of the building. In the restaurant added onto that log house I was confronted with huge collections of corks—a gorgeous tone study of brown to pale ocher circles—from the wine we sold nightly. Once I was old enough to start traveling, I came across so many more circular forms around the world—topiary trees like lollipops in Japan and in formal European gardens; round umbrellas and upside-down flowerpots used as props in display gardens in Amsterdam; round grinding stones set into stone walls in English villages; fountains and mosques in Morocco covered in specially cut tiles to create kaleidoscopic circles and other geometric shapes; bold red circle motifs on Suzani embroideries in Central Asia. The red Suzani circles inspired one of my most popular knitting patterns called Persian Poppy. I led workshops on it where I instructed knitters to tie together random lengths of yarn of different kindred shades to make a big ball of yarn for the poppies and to make another contrasting ball in the same way for the background. Then they just knit away at the simple circle shapes using only these two balls, and each person's effort resulted in a totally unique version of the poppies.

And, of course, the quilting world is chockful of so many real and suggested circles. Yoyos, those rounds of gathered fabric that always remind me of shower caps, add tantalizing texture to quilts. Making thousands of these little circles to sew together could keep an obsessive mind entertained for years. The traditional patchwork block called snowball, created by cutting the corners off a square to make it appear round, is one of my favorite simple illusions. You'll find it on the massive border of Bounce (page 154) and on a larger scale in Floral Snowballs (page 153). The bicycle wheel was a fun motif to play with in the quilt of that name (pages 156 and 157). The quilt was inspired by primitive Indian kantha embroidery. I'm sure decorative artists around the world have for centuries been inspired, like me, by the simple shapes and vibrant colors of objects around them. So intrigued were they by their simplicity and beauty that they spun them endlessly into carvings, weavings, embroideries, and surface decorations.

The little snowball pattern creating a checkerboard on the border of Bounce relates deliciously to the exotic fruits and vegetables I photographed in a market in the hills of Vietnam (opposite page). Their rich tones contrast with the neutral sandy color of the cut-wood box that is such an organic take on circles (above). This reminds us how often the circular form appears in nature.

► BACKGAMMON

In contemplating circles for this book, I recalled the wonderful contrast-color disks of my boyhood board games. The idea to place these circles on a pointed backgammon ground to create this quilt dawned on me as I searched for an alternative to a plain expanse of color.

When Liza and I began this quilt, I was envisioning quite small circles, but when we realized that they were far too fiddly to do by machine, I made them bolder, which I prefer anyway. To keep the circular theme going, we blanket-stitched in contrasting thread around each circle, which reminds me of old-fashioned penny rugs.

I love the chalky, slightly muddy palette here, but another version in bright medium to dark tones would be great, and a strong polka dot in the background would be amusing. This quilt would also be gorgeous in light, dusty pastels. The challenge is to get enough variation in tone and shade to create the little contrasts necessary to separate the circle layers and then to find two different colors for the backgammon background against which those circles will read.

See instructions on pages 158–162.

▲ FLORAL SNOWBALLS

I've been in love with the snowball motif for many years, having come across so many great examples of it in old quilt books and in the work of the Gee's Bend quilters. My favorite in this book is the border of Bounce (page 154), but this large-scale floral version is a joy, too.

A wonderful old door in North London gave me a great curve on which to set this circular design. The door's huge studs create further geometry, and old London brick provides a dark smoldering ground for our deep palette. You could go even darker with this idea: blacks, bottle greens, and dark purples. But lighter tones of ambers, lavenders, and moss greens would also work.

See instructions on pages 163–166.

BOUNCE

Work on this quilt began with the wide "checkerboard" border. I chose many shades of brown, rust, dark pink, and red for my darks; the lights are all the faded soft colors I could find, but not fresh white, as I wanted a vintage feel. The center came later: large circles of print on a dotty background.

Think of all the different treatments you could give this layout by changing the color scheme, such as blue and white or slightly gray pastels with a silvery smoothness to them. Or you could try the whole thing in a collection of different checks and plaids for a very jazzy effect.

Finding a location for this quilt wasn't easy. I tried it on old painted brick walls, in a children's playground with yellow and red painted playing frames, and, finally, on this old, faded blue warehouse with a large round window. It's amazing how many round windows I spotted while doing this research.

See instructions on pages 167–171.

BICYCLE WHEEL

A long time ago, in an exhibition of Indian textiles, I came across some Kantha embroideries with wheel-like motifs stitched with red threads on a cream ground. Later I spotted similar ideas in old quilt books. When I launched into my interpretation, I decided to make the circles dark with glowing two-color borders in order to provide a good field onto which I could embroider my "bicycle spokes." When I do this type of embroidery, I give myself a lot of slack—I don't even attempt uniform stitches—which creates a softer effect than more controlled stitchers would produce. My favorite part of this quilt is the smoldering medium tones of my wheel outlines; those two-color borders really pop out between the black circles and target ground.

See instructions on pages 172–177.

BACKGAMMON

If you like working simple machine-stitched appliqué, this is the quilt for you. Each of the circle motifs is joined together in layers with fusible web before it is stitched in place, so creating the quilt is much easier than it appears. The charming handmade look is achieved by cutting the circles swiftly and not worrying about positioning the layers too precisely.

FINISHED SIZE

54″ × 66″ (135 cm × 165 cm)

MATERIALS

Use quilting cottons 44–45″ (112–114 cm) wide

PATCHWORK FABRICS

Kaffe Fassett *Shot Cottons* (or similar solid-colored fabrics) as follows:

Fabric A (large dark triangles): 1 1/2 yd (1.4 m) of a very dark gray-green—OR *Shot Cotton* in Coal

Fabric B (large green triangles): 3/4 yd (70 cm) each of three different dark-toned greens—OR *Shot Cotton* in Viridian, Moss, and Eucalyptus

Fabric C (border background): 3/4 yd (70 cm) of a dark persimmon red—OR *Shot Cotton* in Bittersweet

Fabric D (circles fabric): 1/4 yd (25 cm) each of 15 different chalky colors, including bright turquoise, tangerine orange, dark rust, light lavender, dark grape, chartreuse, gray-blue, mustard, rose, sky blue, lime, light grass green, bright pink, navy, and lavender—OR *Shot Cotton* in Jade, Tangerine, Cassis, Lavender, Grape, Chartreuse, Smoky, Mustard, Raspberry, Sky Blue, Lime, Grass, Rosy, Navy, and Opal

OTHER INGREDIENTS

Backing fabric: 3 3/4 yd (3.5 m) of desired fabric

Binding fabric: 1/2 yd (46 cm) of a dark grape—OR *Shot Cotton* in Grape

Cotton batting: 61″ × 73″ (150 cm × 180 cm)

Template paper: Pattern paper for making large-triangle templates

Fusible web: 6 yd (5.5 m) of paper-backed iron-on fusible web 17″ (43 cm)

wide, for appliqué motifs (if purchasing wider or narrower fusible web, adjust length)

Appliqué edging thread: Bright orange and fuchsia threads

Quilting thread: Bright orange, fuchsia, and dark green threads

MAKING TEMPLATES

Follow these instructions to make your own templates for the appliqué pieces and the large triangles on this quilt.

QUILT-CENTER TRIANGLES

The triangle templates are very large, so you will need to carefully tape two pieces of paper together, edge to edge. Draw the large whole triangle first—it measures 12″ (30 cm) across the base and is 30″ (75 cm) long. Using a pencil, draw the triangle on the pattern paper, making sure the tip of the triangle is exactly centered on the width of the base. Add a 1/4″ (7.5 mm) seam allowance all around this shape.

Next draw the large half-triangle on the pattern paper—it measures 6″ (15 cm) across the base and is 30″ (75 cm) long. The point of the half-triangle is aligned with one side of the base so that the base has one 90-degree angle. Add a 1/4″ (7.5 mm) seam allowance all around this shape.

Cut out the pattern pieces.

APPLIQUÉ CIRCLES

For the appliqué circles, you will need templates 6″, 5″, 4″, 3″, 2″, and 1″ (15 cm, 12.5 cm, 10 cm, 7.5 cm, 5 cm, and 2.5 cm) in diameter, and some sizes in

The geometry of this old painted house in north London echoes the playful circles on Backgammon. The layered disks with quilted circles are contained by the large half circles at the border. We went for a dark palette, but you could take your cue from the mural and do it in a soft faded colorway.

between these sizes. You can make your own templates out of cardboard, but it is much easier to use items you have at hand, such as saucers, coffee cups, mugs, and jar and pill bottle lids. The only two exact sizes you need, in fact, are 6″ (15 cm) and 3″ (7.5 cm) circle templates; the other sizes can be approximate.

PREPARING APPLIQUÉ FABRIC

Using an iron, fuse the paper-backed adhesive web to the wrong side of the 15 circles fabrics (fabric D), covering only about half of each fabric with the web. Do NOT remove the paper backings. (After cutting the border rectangles and squares from fabric C, prepare the remainder of fabric C in the same way.)

CUTTING PATCHES AND APPLIQUÉ

QUILT CENTER

14 large triangles: Using the pattern piece for the whole triangle, cut six triangles from the very dark fabric (fabric A), three triangles from each of two of the green fabrics (fabric B), and two triangles from the remaining green fabric—for a total of 14 large triangles.

4 large half-triangles: Using the pattern piece for the half-triangle, cut four half-triangles from the very dark fabric (fabric A). (If you are using a fabric with a wrong side and a right side, remember to flop the pattern piece over for two of the half-triangles.)

BORDER

36 rectangles: Cut 36 rectangles measuring 3 1/2″ × 6 1/2″ (9 cm × 16.5 cm) from fabric C.

4 corner squares: Cut four 3 1/2″ (9 cm) squares from fabric C.

APPLIQUÉ MOTIFS

Border half-circles: Using the 6″ (15 cm) circle template, trace circles onto the paper on the wrong side of fabric D. Trace and then cut a total 18 circles this size, making a random number of circles in each color. Then using a range of template sizes from 5″ (12.5 cm) to 2″ (5 cm), trace and cut a total of approximately 50 to 63 circles in a random selection of colors. Next cut all the circles in half for a total of 36 half-circles from the 6″ (15 cm) circles, and a total of 100 to 126 half-circles from the smaller circles. Do NOT remove the paper backings.

Quilt-center circles: Using the 3″ (7.5 cm) circle template, trace circles onto the paper on the wrong side of fabric D. Trace and then cut a total 85 to 90 circles this size, making a random number of circles in each color. Then using a range of template sizes from 2 1/2″ (6.3 cm) to 1″ (2.5 cm), trace and cut a total of 275 to 300 circles in a random selection of colors. Do NOT remove the paper backings.

MAKING LAYERED APPLIQUÉ MOTIFS

Make the appliqué motifs for the quilt center first. Begin by laying out all the 3" (7.5 cm) full circles right side up, with their paper backings still in place.

Then remove the paper backings from all the SMALLER full circles and use these to create layers of circles on top of each of the 3" (7.5 cm) circles. Position at least two and a maximum of four circles on top of each 3" (7.5 cm) circle. When you are satisfied with the color arrangements, fuse each set of layered circles together with an iron. Do not center the circles too precisely on top of each other as the desired effect is a homemade look.

Next lay out all the 6" (15 cm) half-circles right side up, with their paper backings still in place. Remove the paper backings from all the SMALLER half-circles and use these to create layers of half-circles on top of each of the 6" (15 cm) half-circles in the same way as you did for the small full circles. When you are satisfied with the color arrangements, fuse each set of layered half-circles together with an iron.

Using bright orange thread on some circles and fuchsia thread on others, machine-buttonhole-stitch or blanket-stitch around the edge of each of the top layers of circles and half-circles on each of the layered motifs, leaving the outer edge of the base layer raw. Then use tweezers to remove the paper backings from the motifs—this will require patience.

ASSEMBLING QUILT CENTER

To ensure that you match the large fabric triangles correctly when sewing them together, use a pencil to draw the seam line 1/4" (7.5 mm) from the edge on the wrong side of each of the triangle and half-triangle pieces. Then carefully matching the seam lines (especially at the corners), sew the triangles and half-triangles together as shown on the assembly diagram (page 162).

Arrange the layered 3" (7.5 cm) circles on the assembled top, reserving four of these circles for the corners of the borders. Fuse the arranged circles to the background. Using bright orange thread for some motifs and fuchsia thread for others, machine-buttonhole-stitch or blanket-stitch around the outer edge of each of the circles to secure them in place.

ASSEMBLING BORDERS

Place a layered half-circle on each of the 36 border rectangles, center it carefully on the patch, and fuse in place. Fuse a 3" (8 cm) layered circle to each of the four corner squares in the same way. Buttonhole-stitch or blanket-stitch around the outer edge of each half-circle and circle to secure it in place as you did in the quilt center.

Using a 1/4" (7.5 mm) seam allowance, sew the rectangle patches together end to end to form the borders. Sew together eight rectangles for the top and bottom borders, and 10 rectangles for each of the side borders. Sew a corner square to each end of the top and bottom borders.

This photo of an amazing play on circles was found for me, so I'm not exactly sure how it's made. It looks like a mola from South America, but I've never seen one as intensely, finely detailed as this. Suffice it to say, it has a powerful impact and would be an ambitious project to try to emulate as a quilt. I could certainly see it as a needlepoint project or embroidery on a quilt or cushion. The recurring black ground gives the reds, golds, and bright pinks real depth.

Backgammon Assembly

KEY

■ Fabric A

■ ■ ■ Fabric B

■ Fabric C

■ ■ ■ Fabric D

Sew the long border strips to the sides of the quilt center and the short border strips to the top and bottom of the quilt center.

FINISHING QUILT

Press the quilt top. Layer the quilt top, batting, and backing, then baste the layers together (see page 181).

Using bright orange thread or fuchsia thread, machine-quilt around the outer edge (just inside the buttonhole-stitch edging) on each circle and half-circle. Using green thread, machine-quilt circle shapes randomly over the background of the quilt center but not touching the appliqués.

Trim the quilt edges. Then cut the binding fabric on the bias and sew it on around the edge of the quilt (see page 181).

FLORAL SNOWBALLS

To make this design work, keep the contrast between the colors low, using prints with a similar lightness/darkness. The blocks are easy to piece because the tiny corners are stitched on using a simple technique even a beginner can master. Radiating out from the quilt center, the striped border is very effective as it focuses the eye on and emphasizes the circular snowballs.

FINISHED SIZE
93 1/2" × 93 1/2" (238 cm × 238 cm)

MATERIALS
Use quilting cottons 44–45" (112–114 cm) wide

PATCHWORK FABRICS

Fabric A (floral snowballs): 1/2–2 yd (46–180 cm) each of at least 11 different medium-toned to dark-toned large-scale floral prints in magentas, reds, violets, turquoises, verdigris greens, and purples; a total of approximately 11 yd (10 m) —OR the following 11 Kaffe Fassett fabrics:

2 1/2 yd (2.3 m) of *Bekah* in Magenta; 2 yd (1.9 m) of *Bekah* in Plum; 1 1/2 yd (1.4 m) of *Bekah* in Green; 1 1/4 yd (1.2 m) of *Bekah* in Cobalt; 3/4 yd (70 cm) each of *Kimono* in Rust/Purple, Crimson/Magenta, and Cobalt/Turquoise; 1/2 yd (46 cm) each of *Cloisonné* in Aqua and Teal, and of *Lotus Leaf* in Blue and Wine

Fabric B (snowball corners): 3 1/2 yd (3.2 m) of a polka dot print with green dots on a dark burgundy ground—OR Kaffe Fassett *Spot* in Burgundy

Fabric C (border fabric): 1 3/4 yd (1.6 m) of a brown, red, and green print with bands of motifs that form decorative stripes—OR Kaffe Fassett *Jungle Stripe* in Dark

OTHER INGREDIENTS

Backing fabric: 9 yd (8.3 m) of desired fabric

Binding fabric: 1 yd (92 cm) of a solid dark red fabric

Cotton batting: 101" × 101" (255 cm × 255 cm)

Quilting thread: Deep red thread

CUTTING PATCHES

If you are using the suggested Kaffe Fassett fabrics, there is no need to fussy-cut the flowers exactly as they are on our quilt. Frame your large-scale flowers in your own personal way, but to keep the quilt from looking too predictable—and to waste less fabric—cut some of the large squares so that the flower is slightly off center.

229 large floral squares: Centering a flower in each square, fussy-cut 229 patches each 6" (15.5 cm) square from fabric A.

916 small squares for corners: Cut 916 patches each 2 1/4" (6 cm) square from fabric B.

4 border strips: From fabric C, cut four strips each 6" × 83" (15.5 cm × 211.5 cm). (To make long enough strips, cut the strips selvage to selvage and sew together end to end, matching the pattern carefully.)

MAKING BLOCKS

229 blocks: For each of the blocks, you will need to sew one small fabric-B square to each corner of each of the large floral fabric-A squares to form the triangular polka dot corners.

Before stitching the small squares to each block, use a pencil to draw a diagonal line from corner to corner on the wrong side of each of the four small squares (this is the stitching line). Next pin a small square to each of the corners of the large square, with right sides together and with the edges of the fabrics carefully aligned. Stitch each small square in place along the stitching line as shown in step 1 of the diagram for Bounce on page 168. Then trim each seam allowance to 1/4" (7.5 mm) and press the corners back as shown in steps 2 and 3 of the same diagram. Make a total of 229 blocks in this way.

ASSEMBLING TOP

Arrange the quilt center as shown on the assembly diagram (page 166), either laying out the patches on the floor or sticking them to a cotton-flannel design wall. Use 225 blocks to arrange 15 horizontal rows of 15 blocks, setting aside 4 blocks that are nearly identical for the border corners. Keep a nice balance of color.

Using a 1/4" (7.5 mm) seam allowance throughout, sew the blocks together in 15 horizontal rows as shown on the assembly diagram. Then sew the 15 horizontal rows together.

Sew a border strip to each side of the quilt center. Then sew a block to each end of the two remaining border strips. Sew these strips to the top and bottom of the quilt.

FINISHING QUILT

Press the quilt top. Layer the quilt top, batting, and backing, then baste the layers together (see page 181).

Using deep red thread, machine-quilt box shapes in the polka dot corners of the blocks. Then machine-quilt meandering lines around the large flowers, roughly outlining the petals. Lastly, roughly outline the stripes and patterns in the borders.

Trim the quilt edges. Then cut the binding fabric on the bias and sew it on around the edge of the quilt (see page 181).

I'm always amazed when I see how cutting corners off a square gives the illusion of a circle. Then when you fussy-cut or bull's-eye big flowers inside this shape, the circular feeling intensifies. Old London brick walls make a good neutral setting for this fresh palette.

Floral Snowballs Assembly

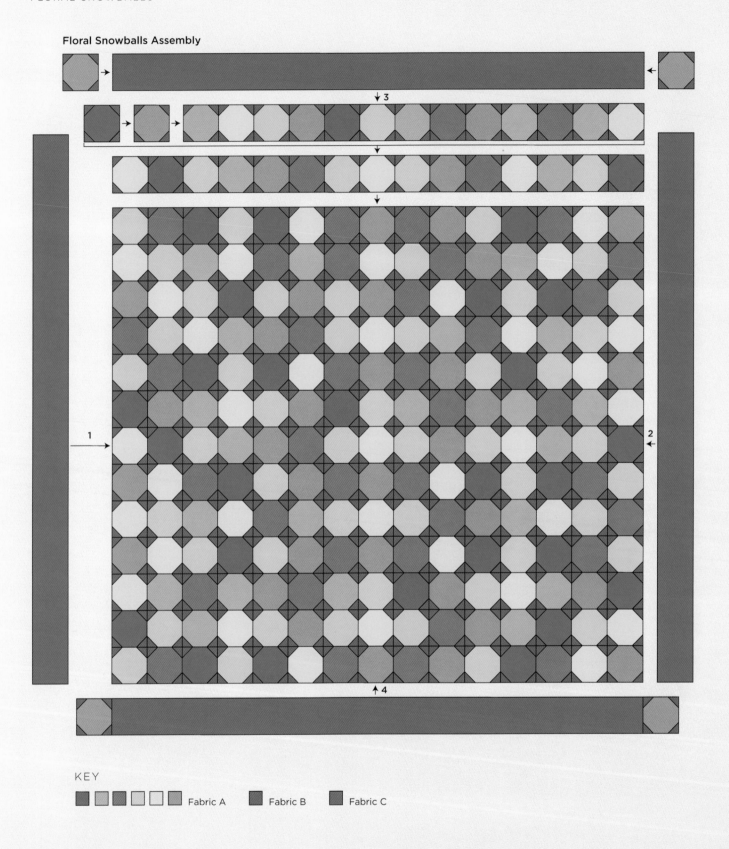

KEY

Fabric A   Fabric B   Fabric C

BOUNCE

Bounce looks like a medley of circular tin can tops, but the border blocks are actually made up of squares with a little triangle at each corner. The large center "bubbles" are appliqué motifs that can be stitched in place by hand or machine. To prevent the background from showing through the appliqué, you simply cut it away behind the bubbles.

FINISHED SIZE
72" × 84" (183 cm × 213.5 cm)

MATERIALS
Use quilting cottons 44–45" (112–114 cm) wide

PATCHWORK FABRICS

Fabric A (quilt center background):
1 1/2 yd (1.4 m) of a print with butter yellow dots and circular flowers on a violet ground—OR Kaffe Fassett *Guinea Flower* in Yellow

Fabric B (center appliqué circles):
Scraps of at least 12 different medium-scale bicolor prints (polka dots, checks, and florals) in blues, muted reds, pinks, golds, and lilacs—OR 1/4 yd (25 cm) each of the following 12 Kaffe Fassett fabrics:

Spot in Lilac and Tomato; *Ikat Polka Dot* in Scarlet, Blue, and Pumpkin; *Silhouette Rose* in Wine, Rose, and Duck Egg; *Ikat Chequerboard* in Navy, Red, and Fuchsia; *Woven Check* in Pink

Fabric C (border darks): 1/4–1/2 yd (25–46 cm) each of at least 12 different medium-dark-toned monochromatic small-scale prints and a few stripes in a fresco palette of plums, rusts, browns, mauves, and muted reds; a total of approximately 2 yd (1.9 m)

Fabric D (border lights): 1/4–1/2 yd (25–46 cm) each of at least 12 different light-toned and medium-light-toned solids, monochromatic small-scale prints, and a few stripes in a fresco palette of dusty

pinks, ecru, duck egg blue, lavenders, and gray-blues; a total of approximately 2 yd (1.9 m)

OTHER INGREDIENTS

Backing fabric: 5 1/2 yd (5 m) of desired fabric

Binding fabric: 3/4 yd (70 cm) of a solid maroon fabric

Cotton batting: 79" × 91" (200 cm × 230 cm)

Quilting thread: Medium beige thread

Templates: Use templates P and R (see page 184)

CUTTING PATCHES

Cut the circle motifs and the background for the quilt center first, then the squares for the border.

QUILT CENTER

Background: From fabric A, cut a rectangle 40" × 52" (102 cm × 132 cm). This background piece will be trimmed to the correct size later after the appliqué circles have been stitched in place.

Bubble motifs: Feel free to make circles of any size using coasters, drinking glasses, small dishes, or bottles; the quilt shown was made with 10 small circles 2 5/8" (6.5 cm) in diameter, four medium-size circles 3 1/2" (9 cm) in diameter, and 14 large circles 6" (15 cm) in diameter—a total of 28 bubbles. To make the circles easier to trace, spray starch the pieces of fabric B and press carefully. Then using a disappearing-ink pen, trace your circles onto the right side of fabric B. Cut the circles out 1/4" (6 mm) from the drawn outline to allow for the hem. Keep these patches flat.

BORDER BLOCKS

480 large squares: Cut 240 large template-P squares from fabric C (darks) and 240 large template-P squares from fabric D (lights)—for a total of 480 squares.

Here we have two deliciously eccentric uses of circles. The installation at the Keukenhof Gardens in Holland is a simple "pavement" made up of upside-down plastic flower pots (above top). Ephemeral yet solid-looking, it made everyone who saw it smile. But for pure bravado the mosaic shown in the photo beneath it takes the cake! It is a detail of artist Evie Ferrier's house in Perth, Australia, which is covered inside and out with brilliant mosaic. I give grateful thanks whenever I come across free spirits like Evie.

1,920 small squares: Cut 240 matching sets of four small template-R squares from fabric C (darks), cutting each set from the same fabric C. Then cut 240 matching sets of four small template-R squares from fabric D (lights), cutting each set from the same fabric D. You will have a total of 1,920 squares (or 480 sets of four).

PREPARING APPLIQUÉ BUBBLES

Turn under the hem around each cut circle, folding along the drawn outline, and baste the hem in place. Press the hemmed circles and set them aside until you are ready to assemble the quilt center.

MAKING BLOCKS

For each of the blocks, you will need to sew one small template-R square to each corner of each of the large template-P squares. Use four matching small template-R squares cut from fabric D (lights) for each large template-P square cut from fabric C (darks), and four matching small template-R squares cut from fabric C (darks) for each large template-P square cut from fabric D (lights).

Before stitching the small squares to each block, use a pencil to draw a diagonal line from corner to corner on the wrong side of each of the four small squares (this is shown as the stitching line on template R). Next pin a small square to each of the corners of the large square, with right sides together and with the edges of the fabrics carefully aligned. Stitch each small square in place along the stitching line as shown in step 1 of the block diagram. Then trim each seam allowance to 1/4" (6 mm) and press the corners back as shown in steps 2 and 3.

Bounce Block

Step 1
Stitch.

Step 2
Trim.

Step 3
Press corners back.

Make a total of 480 blocks—240 with a dark (fabric-C) center and light (fabric-D) triangle corners, and 240 with a light (fabric-D) center and dark (fabric-C) triangle corners.

ASSEMBLING TOP

Assemble the quilt center first, then add the border blocks.

Bounce Assembly

KEY

Fabric A   Fabric B   Fabric C   Fabric D

QUILT CENTER

Draw a rectangle 36″ × 48″ (91.4 cm × 121.9 cm) on the background fabric (fabric A), using chalk or a disappearing-ink pen. (This is a temporary outline of the finished size of the center to help guide the placement of the bubbles.) Place the prepared appliqué bubbles on the background fabric, keeping them within the drawn outline. They should be scattered randomly. Pin the bubbles to the background and appliqué them in place around the edge by hand or machine.

When all the bubbles are sewn to the background, remove the basting threads. Then carefully cut away the background fabric behind each bubble, leaving a 1/4″ (6 mm) seam allowance. Press the assembled quilt center well. The appliqué will have caused the background to shrink a little, so ignore the previously drawn outline, measure the background again, and trim it to 36 1/2″ × 48 1/2″ (92 cm × 122.5) to allow for the seam allowances.

BLOCK BORDERS

Arrange the border blocks as shown on the assembly diagram (page 170), either laying them out on the floor or sticking them to a cotton-flannel design wall.

For the top border, arrange six horizontal rows of 24 blocks, alternating the light and dark blocks to achieve the correct effect.

For each side border, arrange six vertical rows of 16 blocks, alternating the light and dark blocks. (Make sure that the light and dark blocks will alternate correctly where they meet up with the blocks of the top border.)

Arrange the bottom border as for the top border.

Using the seam allowance marked on the templates throughout, first sew the blocks together in rows, then sew the rows together as shown on the assembly diagram.

Sew the side borders to the quilt center, then sew on the top and bottom borders.

FINISHING QUILT

Press the quilt top. Layer the quilt top, batting, and backing, then baste the layers together (see page 181).

Using medium beige thread, machine-quilt a 2–3″ (5–7.5 cm) circle in the center of each appliqué circle in the quilt center, then one or two more concentric circles between the center circle and the edge of the motif—think tin can tops! Lastly, machine-quilt spirals in the background of the quilt center, and a spiral in each square and circle of the border.

Trim the quilt edges. Then cut the binding fabric and sew it on around the edge of the quilt (see page 181).

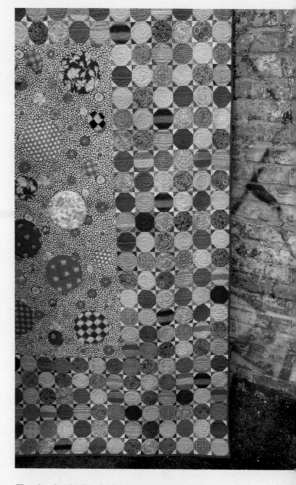

The idea for this border came from a quilt from 1875 I spotted in an old quilt book. It was mostly red and white, with brown, sky blue, and yellow softening the crispness. The little corner triangles creating a sort of pinwheel are what made me want to reproduce it. My version is less contrasting but gives off a warmer radiance thanks to the medium tones I used. The stripes in the quilt all run horizontally, which helps maintain a sense of order in the scrappiness of it all, as do the closely toned fabrics.

BICYCLE WHEEL

This quilt is very easy and quick to stitch since it is composed of a large center background fabric and wide inner and outer borders. The rims on the bicycle wheels are made with a simple technique called paper foundation piecing, which is explained in full in the instructions. The spokes on the wheels are embroidered by hand in chain-stitch.

FINISHED SIZE
58" × 78" (147 cm × 198 cm)

MATERIALS
Use quilting cottons 44–45" (112–114 cm) wide

PATCHWORK FABRICS

Fabric A (center background): 2 1/2 yd (2.3 m) of a dark-medium-toned large-scale target-circles print in cobalt blue, wine, ocher, cool green, and charcoal—OR Kaffe Fassett *Targets* in Green

Fabric B (wheel centers): 1/2 yd (46 cm) each of five different dark-toned fabrics (two monochromatic circles prints, one check, one stripe, and one polka dot) in chocolate brown, lapis blue, wines, and black—OR 1/2 yd (46 cm) each of the five following Kaffe Fassett fabrics:

Aboriginal Dot in Chocolate and Periwinkle; *Two-Toned Stripe* in Burgundy; *Spot* in Black; and *Woven Check* in Burgundy

Fabric C (wheel rims): 1/4 yd (25 cm) each of 10 different medium-toned fabrics (five dot prints and five monochromatic prints) in pinks, scarlet, wine, cool greens, purple, and dark lime—OR 1/4 yd (25 cm) each of the 10 following Kaffe Fassett fabrics:

Spot in Purple, Green, Burgundy, and Red; *Printed Ikat Polka Dot* in Scarlet; *Aboriginal Dot* in Red and Orange; and *Stencil Carnation* in Green, Malacite, and Rose

Fabric D (inner border): 1 3/4 yd (1.6 m) of a large-scale check in tangerine and bottle green—OR Kaffe Fassett *Ikat Chequerboard* in Gold

Fabric E (outer border): 3 yd (2.8 m) of a print with large circular motifs in medium-toned bright colors on a black ground—OR Kaffe Fassett *Turkish Delight* in Jewel

OTHER INGREDIENTS

Backing fabric: 4 yd (3.7 m) of desired fabric

Binding fabric: 3/4 yd (70 cm) of a blue monochromatic print

Cotton batting: 65" × 85" (165 cm × 215 cm)

Appliqué thread: Bright variegated bright red/orange thread

Embroidery thread (bicycle spokes): Stranded cotton embroidery floss in pale yellow, bright yellow, pale pink, bright pink, pale orange, bright orange, and red

Quilting thread: Medium taupe thread

Templates: Use templates S and T (page 191)

SPECIAL FABRIC NOTE

When making the wheels for the quilt, use a different fabric B for each of the centers and fabric C for the rims. The rim on each wheel is made up of two different contrasting fabrics. If you are using the Kaffe Fassett fabrics listed for the wheels and rims, you can mix the fabrics as you wish or use the combinations on the actual quilt, counting the wheels from the top to bottom and left to right as follows:

Wheel 1: For the wheel center, *Aboriginal Dot* in Chocolate; and for the wheel rim, *Aboriginal Dot* in Orange and *Spot* in Purple.

Wheel 2: For the wheel center, *Aboriginal Dot* in Periwinkle; and for the wheel rim, *Spot* in Green and *Printed Ikat Polka Dot* in Scarlet.

Wheel 3: For the wheel center, *Two-Toned Stripe* in Burgundy; and for the wheel rim, *Spot* in Burgundy and *Aboriginal Dot* in Red.

Wheel 4: For the wheel center, *Spot* in Black; and for the wheel rim, *Spot* in Red and *Stencil Carnation* in Green.

Wheel 5: For the wheel center, *Woven Check* in Burgundy; and for the wheel rim, *Stencil Carnation* in Malacite and Rose.

The cushion above is another of my textile finds. I got it for 5 pounds at an antique fabric fair in Manchester. Although I usually don't care that much for tricky folded fabric, the soft palette of this cushion attracted me. The stone pavement in the photo beneath the cushion is so exciting because it is broken up into dynamic circles—thank you for making the creative effort, whoever you are. These simple wheel-like circles abound in our surroundings, so try keeping a lookout for them to feed your design ideas.

CUTTING PATCHES

Cut all the patches for the quilt as explained here, except for the wheel rims, which are made with the paper foundation piecing method.

QUILT CENTER

Background: From fabric A, cut a piece 40 1/2" × 60 1/2" (103.5 cm × 154.5 cm).

20 template-T wheel-center patches: For the five wheel centers, cut four template-T quarter circles from each of the five wheel fabrics (fabric B)—for a total of 20 quarter circles.

INNER BORDER

4 border strips: From fabric D, cut two strips 3 1/2" × 60 1/2" (9 cm × 154.5 cm) for the side borders; then cut two strips 3 1/2" × 40 1/2" (9 cm × 103.5 cm) for the top and bottom borders. Center the check pattern within these border strips.

4 corner squares: From fabric A, fussy-cut four squares 3 1/2" × 3 1/2" (9 cm × 9 cm), centering a target-circle within each square.

OUTER BORDER

4 border strips: From fabric E, cut two strips 6 1/2" × 46 1/2" (16.5 cm × 118.5 cm) for the top and bottom borders; then cut two strips 6 1/2" × 66 1/2" (16.5 cm × 169.5 cm) for the side borders. Center the print pattern within these border strips, matching the opposite sides as closely as possible to each other. (To make long enough matching strips from the large-scale print, cut the strips selvage to selvage and sew together end to end, matching the pattern carefully.)

4 corner squares: From fabric A, fussy-cut four squares 6 1/2" × 6 1/2" (16.5 cm × 16.5 cm), centering a target-circle within each square.

MAKING FOUNDATION-PIECED WHEEL RIMS

The wheel rim patches are sewn together with the easy paper foundation piecing technique. For this, each rim block requires a paper foundation. Make four photocopies of rim template S (see page 191) for each of the five bicycle wheels on the quilt—a total of 20 photocopies. (Do not photocopy a photocopy because this can distort the very accurate size of the design.) Cut out each paper foundation exactly around the outer line, including the seam allowance on three sides (there is no seam allowance at the outside edge of the rim-block paper foundation).

PREPARING PATCHES

To begin the first rim block, first choose two different rim fabrics (fabric C) for the patches (see Special Fabric Note, page 172). Roughly cut a fabric piece for each numbered area of the foundation, four patches in each of the two colors; allow at least 1/2" (12 mm) extra fabric all around the edge of the patch area on the paper foundation. For each of these eight rim patches, a piece about 2 1/2" (6.5 cm) square will be big enough. There is no need to pay attention to the

Bicycle Wheel Assembly

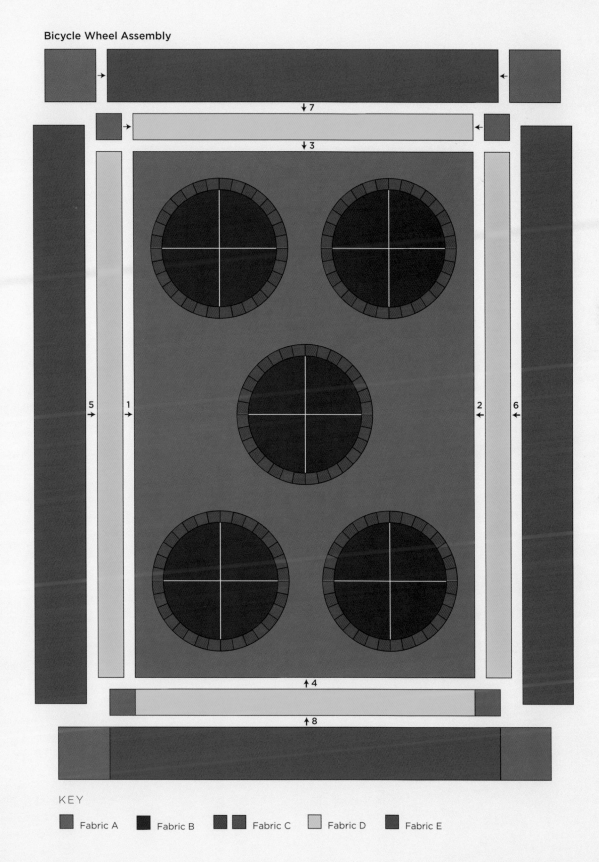

KEY

Fabric A   Fabric B   Fabric C   Fabric D   Fabric E

Paper Foundation Piecing

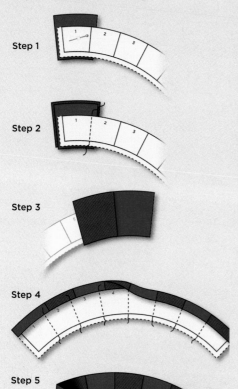

Step 1

Step 2

Step 3

Step 4

Step 5

Bicycle Wheel Block

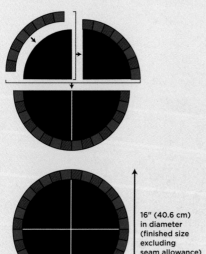

16" (40.6 cm) in diameter (finished size excluding seam allowance)

fabric grain line when cutting and stitching the patches, because the paper foundation they are being stitched onto will provide the necessary stability.

STITCHING FIRST RIM BLOCK

Insert a 90/14 needle in your sewing machine and set it to a short stitch—the large needle and short stitch will help perforate the paper and make it easy to tear it away later.

Place the roughly cut patch for section no. 1 behind the paper with the wrong side facing the paper (see step 1). Make sure the fabric covers the patch area outlined by the solid line and extends about 1/2" (12 mm) beyond it, then pin it in position.

Place the patch for section no. 2 behind the first patch with the right sides of the fabrics together. With the paper still facing upward, sew the two patches together along the stitching line between the two sections, stitching through the paper and the two layers of fabric (see step 2). Begin and end the stitching slightly beyond each end of the seam line; this stitching will be secured by future seams.

Trim the seam allowance to 1/4" (6 mm) on the seam just stitched. Open out patch no. 2 and finger press the seam (see step 3). Then press the seam with a hot iron but no steam. Add all the remaining pieces in the same way, stitching them on in the sequence indicated by the numbers.

FINISHING FIRST RIM BLOCK

Once all the patches have been stitched in place and pressed, trim the fabric to the edge of the paper foundation along the inside edge and the two short sides. Along the outside edge of the rim, trim the fabric to within 1/2" (12 mm) of the paper and fold this edge over to the front of the numbered side of the paper and press (see steps 4 and 5). Machine-baste this turned-down edge to the paper, stitching between the seam lines at each short end but not into the seam allowance.

MAKING REMAINING RIM BLOCKS

Make three more rims like the first for the first wheel. Then make four rim blocks for each of the remaining five wheels, using two different colors for each set of four. Once you have a total of 20 completed rim blocks, you are ready to begin making the wheels.

MAKING BICYCLE WHEEL BLOCKS

To make the first bicycle wheel block, take one set of four matching template-T quarter circles and one set of four matching rim blocks. On one rim block, tear away the paper about halfway up from the inner edge of the rim and away from both sides so that the paper will not be caught in the seams. Be sure to leave the paper in place along the machine-basted outer edge of the rim.

Pin this rim to a quarter circle, clipping and notching the seam allowance as necessary, and sew in place. Press.

Sew the three remaining rim blocks to the three remaining quarter circles of this first bicycle wheel. Then sew the four prepared quarters together as shown in the block diagram to complete the first wheel.

Using heavy starch, spray the wheel and press, making sure that the outside edge of the wheel is especially well sprayed and pressed. Gently remove the basting stitches and the rest of the paper on the wrong side of the wheel.

Make the remaining four wheel blocks in the same way.

ASSEMBLING TOP

Arrange the wheel blocks on the quilt center background as shown in the assembly diagram (page 175), placing one in the exact center and the remaining four approximately 3 1/2" (9 cm) from the top or bottom edges and 2 1/4" (6 cm) from the side edges. Machine-baste the wheels in position around the rim, then machine-blanket-stitch in place around the outer edge using variegated bright red/orange thread.

Before adding the borders, embroider spokes on each of the wheels. Using two strands of cotton embroidery floss and random colors (see Materials list), first work a circle 1 1/2—2 1/4" (4–6 cm) in diameter at the center of the wheel. Then embroider the spokes, chain-stitching 32 equally spaced straight lines from the center circle to the rim.

Using a 1/4" (7.5 mm) seam allowance throughout, sew one of the long inner-border strips to each side of the quilt center. Then sew one inner-border square to each end of the two short inner-border strips and stitch these borders to the top and bottom of the quilt.

Sew on the outer borders in the same way, then remove the basting stitches on the wheels.

FINISHING QUILT

Press the quilt top. Layer the quilt top, batting, and backing, then baste the layers together (see page 181).

Using medium taupe thread, stitch-in-the-ditch around each side of each wheel rim and around each side of the inner border. Next machine-quilt straight lines along each side of each embroidered spoke on the wheels and concentric circles about 2" (5 cm) apart on the background fabric circle motifs and the border corner squares. Then machine-quilt two wavy lines along the center of the inner border and outline-quilt around the large motifs in the outer border.

Trim the quilt edges. Then cut the binding fabric on the bias and sew it on around the edge of the quilt (see page 181).

I once did a vast mosaic mural for a Scottish pottery using large circles of striped plates. This gave me the idea to create a circular fabric for patchworkers to cut up in the same way. I called it Targets and it made a perfect ground for Bicycle Wheel.

BASIC TECHNIQUES

If you are an absolute beginner but are a proficient sewer, you should be able tackle most of the quilts in this book. For a little support, however, you may want to take an introductory class or have an experienced quilter guide you through your first project.

This chapter can't begin to cover all of the many quilting shortcuts, but the tips provided should make the patchwork and quilting process easier and more fun. Don't get too worried about technique when you begin. Some of the most wonderful museum quilts have imperfect stitching lines that add to their homemade charm. Concentrate instead on the beautiful colors you are using and on composing them into a spectacular quilt.

FABRIC

Pure, lightweight cotton known as quilting cotton is best. It is firmly woven, and so easy to cut, crease, and press, but it is slow to fray. Quilting cotton comes in a seemingly endless range of colors and prints, which means you can create a quilt with any palette you like.

USING SCRAP FABRICS

My designs are especially suited to the use of scrap fabrics—pieces big enough for several patches. This is because I like to include lots of slightly different shades in any color scheme and often use a variety of prints, stripes, and solids as well. So if you have a large collection of scraps, you may already have almost enough fabric to make a Kaffe Fassett quilt. You can supplement your scraps by buying small lengths of any colors you are missing and even add in scraps cut from old dresses, blouses, or shirts. Just be sure to use only 100-percent cotton fabrics in a weight similar to that of standard quilting cotton.

CHOOSING FABRIC COLORS AND PRINTS

The instructions for each of the quilts in this book provide general descriptions of the types of fabrics you will need for the quilt—for example, prints, stripes, or solids. They also outline the general color scheme. For some quilts, Kaffe Fassett or Rowan fabrics are listed for the entire quilt or for parts of the quilt; these, however, may not be available by the time you decide to make a particular quilt. Don't let this deter you—the clear guidelines for fabric colors and prints will allow you to select all you need to make a similar quilt. And the most fun part of quilting, I believe, is playing with and mixing fabric colors and prints and finding a palette that really sings.

When choosing your fabrics, pay particular attention to the lightness or darkness of the colors, which is also explained in the fabric groups listed for the quilt. My quilts usually have a fairly subtle contrast in the lights and darks used. So remember that if one fabric group requires "light-toned" prints and the other "dark-toned" prints, you may be able to use medium tones instead of very light tones in the "lights" group; the patchwork geometry will work as long as the "darks" are slightly darker than the "lights." Closeness in tone, rather than sharp tonal contrast, creates a composition of great richness and hidden depths. If you study your favorite antique quilts you will see they often use very restrained light–dark contrasts.

Always look carefully at the photograph of the quilt as you choose your fabric palette. Notice the scale of the prints and the types of prints as well. Very small-scale prints can look like solids at a distance, but provide more interest and visual "texture" than solids. Large-scale prints are particularly useful because you can cut completely different colors from different areas of the same fabric. Dots and stripes, even used in only a few areas of a quilt, add amazing movement to the composition.

When choosing multicolored prints, study them at a distance. Looking at them up close, you may think you are choosing a particular color, but at a distance they turn into something totally different. For example, you may think you are choosing a "red" because there are bright red small-scale motifs on a white ground, but at a distance it looks pink! Similarly, motifs in two different colors will blend together at a distance to make a totally new color; for example, separate blues and yellows on the same print will make it look green.

If you are in doubt, buy small amounts of fabrics and test them by cutting and arranging some patches and then standing back to see the effect at a distance.

DETERMINING HOW MUCH FABRIC YOU NEED

Determining fabric amounts for my designs is not an exact science because I use so many different fabrics. The quantities in the instructions are only an approximate guide. Of course, it is better to have too much fabric than too little, and you can always use the leftovers for future projects.

If you do run out of fabric, it is not a tragedy. I think of it as a design opportunity! The replacement you find may make the quilt look even better. After all, quiltmaking originated as a way to use up scraps, and chance combinations of fabrics sometimes resulted in antique masterpieces.

When calculating exact fabric amounts for borders, bindings, or backings on your own designs, remember that although quilting cottons are usually 44" to 45" (about 112 cm to 114 cm) wide, the usable width is sometimes only about 40" to 42" (102 cm to 107 cm) due to slight shrinkage and the removal of selvages.

PREPARING PATCHWORK FABRIC

Always prewash your fabrics before use. This will confirm colorfastness and preshrink the fabric just in case it may be prone to this. Wash the darks and lights separately and rinse them well. Then press the fabric with a hot iron while it is still damp. After pressing, cut off the selvages; you can do this quickest with a rotary cutter.

TOOLS AND EQUIPMENT

If you have a sewing machine, you probably already have most of the tools necessary for making quilts in your sewing box. Aside from the sewing machine, you'll need fabric scissors, pins, needles, a ruler, a pencil, an ironing board, and an iron. Nothing more is needed for making a simple patchwork made entirely of squares.

For other patch shapes, you will need templates. Premade templates in standard sizes are readily available, and nonstandard sizes and shapes can be made easily from cardboard or special template plastic.

The most useful additional tools—the ones that no modern-day patchworker could do without—are a rotary cutter, a rotary-cutting mat, and a rotary-cutting ruler. With these you can cut your patches quickly and accurately in straight lines.

DESIGN WALL AND REDUCING GLASS

If you're serious about quilting, I strongly recommend a design wall and a reducing glass. A full-size quilt can be arranged on the floor, but it is much easier to view on a wall. Our design wall is large enough for a queen-size bedcover and is made with two sheets of insulation board, each measuring 4 feet by 8 feet (about 122 cm by 244 cm). Insulation board is a very light board about 3/4" (2 cm) thick; it has a foam core that is covered on one side with paper and on the other with foil. Any sturdy, lightweight board like this will do, but insulation board is especially handy because it can be cut with a craft knife.

To make a design wall, cover each of the two boards on one side with a good-quality cotton flannel in a neutral color such as dull light brown, taupe, or medium gray. Then join the boards with three "hinges" of strong adhesive tape, sticking the hinges to the back of the boards so that you can fold the flannel sides together. The tape hinges will also allow you to bend the design wall slightly so it will stand by itself. If you want to put the wall away with a design in progress on it, just place paper over the arranged patches, fold the boards together, and slide them under a bed.

A quilter's reducing glass looks like a magnifying glass, but instead of making things look larger it makes them look smaller. Looking at a fabric or a design in progress through a reducing glass helps you see how the fabric print or even a whole patchwork layout will look at a distance. Seeing your quilt layout reduced makes any errors in color or pattern pop out and become very obvious. Reducing glasses are usually available in shops that sell patchwork and quilting supplies. A camera isn't quite as good, but it is an acceptable substitute.

PREPARING PATCHES

Once you have prepared all the fabrics for your quilt, you are ready to start cutting patches. Square patches, rectangle patches, and simple half-square triangle patches can be cut quickly and accurately with a rotary cutter, but you will need to use scissors for more complicated shapes.

USING A ROTARY CUTTER

Rotary cutting is really useful for cutting accurate square patches and quilt border strips. Having a range of large and small cutting mats and rotary-cutting rulers is handy, but if you want to start out with just one mat and one ruler, buy an 18" by 24" (46 cm by 61 cm) mat and a 6" by 24" (15 cm by 61 cm) ruler. The ruler will have measurements markings on it as well as 90-, 60-, and 45-degree angles.

If you have never used a rotary cutter before, ask a friend or someone at the store where you buy it to demonstrate how it works, paying particular attention to safety advice. Always use the cutter in conjunction with a cutting mat and a rotary-cutting ruler. You press down on the ruler and the cutter and roll the cutter away from you along the edge of the ruler.

With a little practice, you will be able to cut patches very quickly with a rotary cutter. Long strips can be cut from folded fabric, squares from long strips, and half-square triangles from squares. Just remember to change the cutter blade as soon as it shows the slightest hint of dulling.

MAKING TEMPLATES

Templates for the quilts in this book are provided on pages 182–191. Photocopy them and cut them out before you begin your quilt. If the shapes can be cut quickly with a rotary cutter, use the templates as a guide to your rotary cutting. If not, you can make cardboard or plastic templates from them and trace around them.

Special translucent template plastic makes the best templates. It is very durable and retains its shape even when traced around repeatedly. It is also handy because of its transparency—you can see through it to frame fabric motifs.

It is a good idea to punch a hole in each corner of your template at each pivot point on the seam line, using a 1/8" (3 mm) hole punch. This will increase the accuracy of your seam lines, especially on diamonds and triangles.

Before going on to cut all your patches, make a patchwork block with test pieces to check the accuracy of the templates.

CUTTING TEMPLATE PATCHES

To cut patches using a template, place the template face down on the wrong side of the fabric and align the fabric grain line arrow with the straight grain of the fabric (the crosswise or the lengthwise grain). Pressing the template down firmly with one hand, draw around it with a sharp pencil in the other hand. To save fabric, position the patches as close together as possible or even touching.

CUTTING REVERSE TEMPLATE PATCHES

A reverse template is the mirror image of the patch shape. A template that is marked as a template and a reverse template can be used for both shapes. For the reverse shape, lay the template face up (instead of face down) on the wrong side of the fabric, and draw around it in the usual way.

SEWING PATCHES TOGETHER

Quilt instructions include a layout diagram that shows you how to arrange the various patch shapes to form the quilt design. Often several patches are joined together to form small blocks and then the finished blocks are sewn together to form the whole quilt. Whether you are arranging a block or a whole quilt, lay the patches out on the floor or stick them to a design wall (see Tools and Equipment). Then study the effect of your arrangement carefully, stepping back to look at it or looking at it through a reducing glass.

Only stitch pieces together once you are sure the color arrangement is just right. If you are unsure, leave it for a few days and see how you feel when you come back. If you're still not sure, try another arrangement, or try replacing colors that do not seem to work together with new shades. Remember that an unpredictable arrangement will have more energy and life than one that follows a strict light/dark geometry.

MACHINE-STITCHING STRAIGHT SEAMS

Sew, or piece, patches together following the order specified in the instructions. Use the same neutral-colored thread to piece the entire patchwork. I find that medium taupe or medium gray thread works well for most quilts unless the overall palette is very light, in which case I use ecru thread.

Pin the patches together with right sides facing and match the seam lines and corner points carefully. (If you are proficient at the sewing machine, you will be able to stitch small squares together without pinning.) As you machine-stitch the seam, remove each pin before the needle reaches it. Always stitch from raw edge to raw edge, except on inset seams. There is no need to work backstitches at the beginning and end of each patch seam because the stitches will be secured by crossing seam lines as the pieces are joined together.

To save time and thread, you can chain piece the patch. To do this, feed through the pinned-together pieces one after another without lifting the presser foot; the machine will stitch through nothing a few times before it reaches the next pair of patches. Simply clip the chain of patches apart when you're finished.

PRESSING PATCH SEAMS

Press all seams flat to embed the stitches. Then open out the patches and press the seam allowances to one side. As you continue stitching patches into blocks, then the blocks into rows as instructed, press the seam allowances in each row (of patches or blocks) in the same direction. Press the seam allowances in every alternate row in the opposite direction to avoid having to stitch through two layers of seam allowances at once when joining the rows together.

STITCHING INSET SEAMS

Most of the quilts in this book are made with simple, easy-to-stitch straight seams. But a couple require inset seams—these are seams that turn a corner.

To sew an inset seam, first align the patches along one side of the angle and pin, matching the corner points of the patches exactly. Machine-stitch along the seam line of this edge up to the corner point and work a few backstitches to secure. Then pivot the set-in patch, align the next side with the edge of the adjacent patch, and pin. Beginning exactly at the corner point, work a few backstitches to secure, then machine-stitch along the seam line.

Trim away excess fabric from the seam allowance at the corner of the inset patch as necessary. Then, easing the corner into the correct shape, press the new seams.

QUILTING AND FINISHING

After you have finished piecing your quilt, press it carefully. It is now ready to be quilted. Quilting is the allover stitching that joins together the three layers of the quilt sandwich—patchwork top, batting, and backing.

I often use stitch-in-the-ditch machine-quilting for my quilts. In this type of quilting, the stitching lines are worked very close to the patch seams and are invisible on the right side of the quilt. Echo-quilting is another simple quilting pattern that suits many patchwork designs; it is worked by stitching 1/4" (6 mm) inside the patch seam lines to echo the shape of the patch. Another one of my favorites is outlining motifs on large-scale prints with quilting stitches.

More complicated quilting patterns can be marked on the quilt before you machine-stitch them. Quilting stores sell quilting stencils for these.

Test your chosen quilting on a spare pieced block, stitching through all three quilt layers. This is also a good way to check whether the color of the quilting thread is suitable. The thread color should usually blend invisibly into the overall color of the quilt when it is viewed from a distance.

PREPARING THE QUILT BACKING AND BATTING

Before you quilt your patchwork, you need to prepare the two other layers. Choose a backing fabric that will not do a disservice to the quilt top. Liza likes using half-price fabrics for backings, but they still have to have a certain charm of their own and go well with the patchwork top.

Cut the selvages off the backing fabric, then seam the pieces together to form a backing at least 3" (7.5 cm) bigger all around than the patchwork top.

Batting comes in various thicknesses. Pure cotton or mixed cotton and polyester batting, which is fairly thin, is a good choice for most quilts. Thicker batting is usually only suitable when the quilt layers are being tied together with little knots rather than quilting. I prefer pure cotton batting because it gives a quilt the attractive, relatively flat appearance of an antique quilt.

If the batting has been rolled, unroll it and let it rest before cutting it to about the same size as the backing.

BASTING TOGETHER THE QUILT LAYERS

To keep the three layers of the quilt firmly in place during the quilting process, baste them together. Lay out the backing, wrong side up, and place the batting on top of it. Lay the finished, pressed patchwork, right side up, on top of the batting, and make sure the layers are smoothed out.

Beginning at the center for each stitching line, baste two diagonal lines from corner to corner through the layers of the quilt. Work stitches about 3" (7.5 cm) long and try not to lift the layers too much as you stitch. Always beginning at the center and working outward, baste horizontal and vertical lines about 6" (15 cm) apart across the layers.

MACHINE-QUILTING

For machine-quilting, use a walking foot for straight lines and a darning foot for curved lines. Choose a color that blends with the overall color of the patchwork for the top thread and one that matches the backing for the bobbin thread. Follow the sewing machine manual for tips on using the walking or darning feet.

BINDING QUILT EDGES

When the quilting is finished, remove the basting threads. Trim away the excess batting and backing right up to the edge of the patchwork, straightening the edge of the patchwork at the same time, if necessary.

Cut 2" (5 cm)-wide binding strips either on the straight grain or on the bias. To make a strip long enough to fit around the edge of the quilt, sew these strips end to end, joining bias strips with diagonal seams. Fold the strip in half lengthwise with the wrong sides together and press.

Place the doubled binding on the right side of the quilt, with the right sides facing and the raw edges of both layers of the binding aligned with the raw edges of the quilt. Machine-stitch 1/4" (6 mm) from the edge and stitch up to 1/4" (6 mm) from the first corner. Make a few backstitches and cut the thread ends. Then fold the binding upward so that it makes a 45-degree angle at the corner of the quilt. Keeping the diagonal fold just made in place, fold the binding back down and align the edges with the next side of the quilt. Beginning at the point where the last stitching ended, stitch down the next side to within 1/4" (6 mm) of the next corner, and so on. When you reach the beginning of the binding, turn under the edge of one end and tuck the other end inside it.

Turn the folded edge of the binding to the back of the quilt and hand-stitch it in place, folding a miter at each corner.

TEMPLATES

Most of the templates for the quilts are included actual size. If the templates are too large to fit in the book actual size, they have either been reduced or only half of the template is provided.

The solid lines on the templates represent the seam lines and the dotted lines the seam allowances. The arrows on the templates indicate the direction of the fabric grain line.

TUMBLING FANS

See pages 138–143 for Tumbling Fans. The four templates (M, M reverse, O, N) for this quilt are shown here actual size. Templates M and M reverse are photocopied to make the paper foundation pieces needed for the fan blocks (note that the stitching lines between patches no. 1 and no. 2 and between patches no. 2 and no. 3 on the paper foundation piece do not extend all the way to the point of the triangular block). Template N is an appliqué template.

**Flop template O for O reverse.

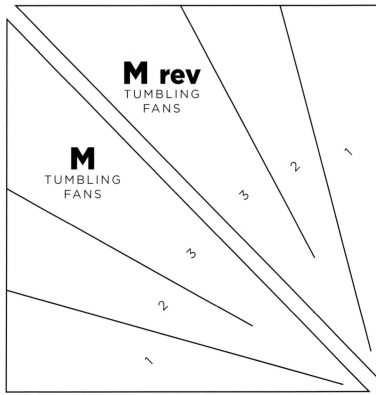

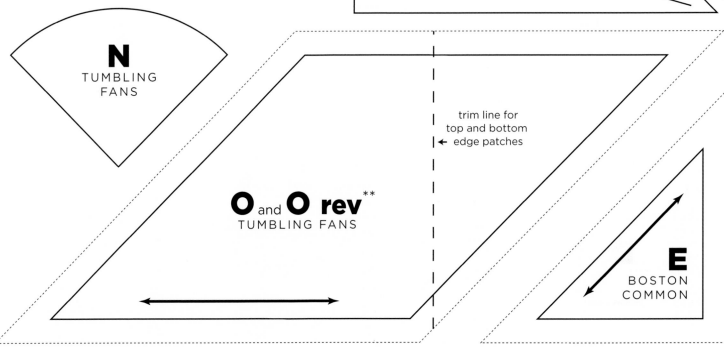

BOSTON COMMON

See pages 20–25 for Boston Common. The three templates (C, D, E) for this quilt are shown here actual size.

STRIPED DONUT

See pages 26–30 for Striped Donut. The six templates (AA, BB, CC, DD, EE, FF) for this quilt are shown here actual size. Templates AA, DD, EE, and FF are all used to cut patches from striped fabrics; when using these templates, remember that the stripes on the fabrics should run in the same direction as the grain-line marker (the arrow).

**Flop templates EE and FF for templates EE reverse and FF reverse. It is important to use reverse EE and reverse FF where indicated in the instructions so the stripes run in the correct direction.

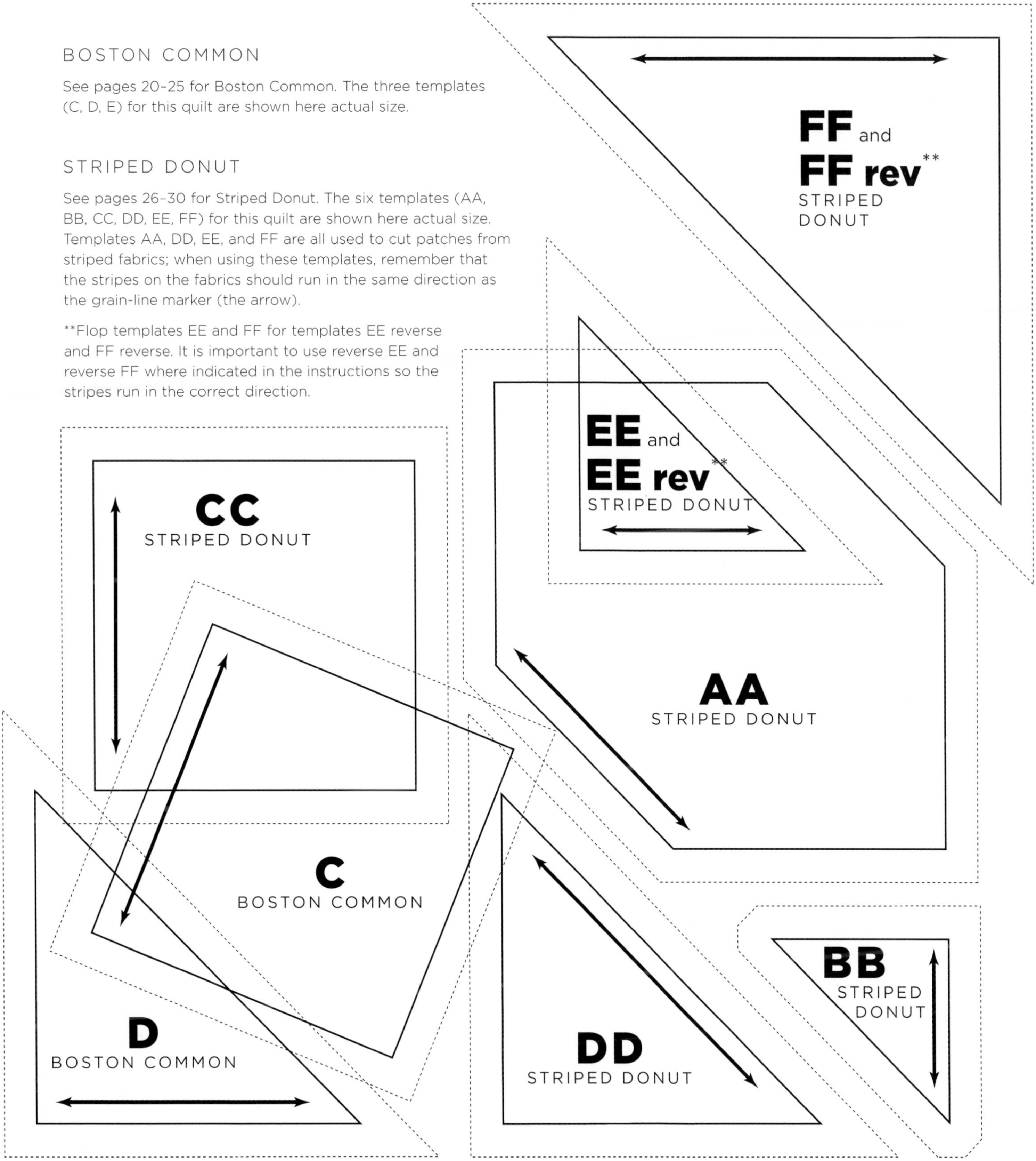

FF and
FF rev**
STRIPED DONUT

EE and
EE rev**
STRIPED DONUT

AA
STRIPED DONUT

CC
STRIPED DONUT

C
BOSTON COMMON

D
BOSTON COMMON

DD
STRIPED DONUT

BB
STRIPED DONUT

TILT

See pages 46–49 for Tilt. The four templates (GG, HH, JJ, KK) for this quilt are shown here (and on the next page) actual size.

BOW-TIE CIRCLES

See pages 144–147 for Bow-Tie Circles. The two templates (P, Q) for this quilt are shown here actual size.

BOUNCE

See pages 167–171 for Bounce. The two templates (R, P) for this quilt are shown here actual size.

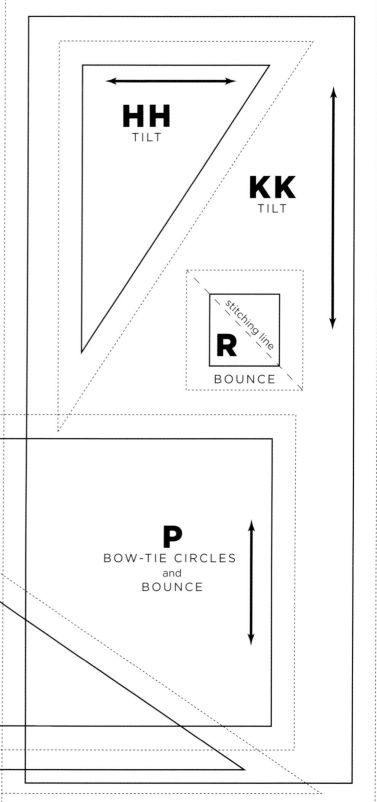

HH
TILT

KK
TILT

R
BOUNCE
stitching line

Q
BOW-TIE CIRCLES
stitching line

P
BOW-TIE CIRCLES
and
BOUNCE

JJ
TILT

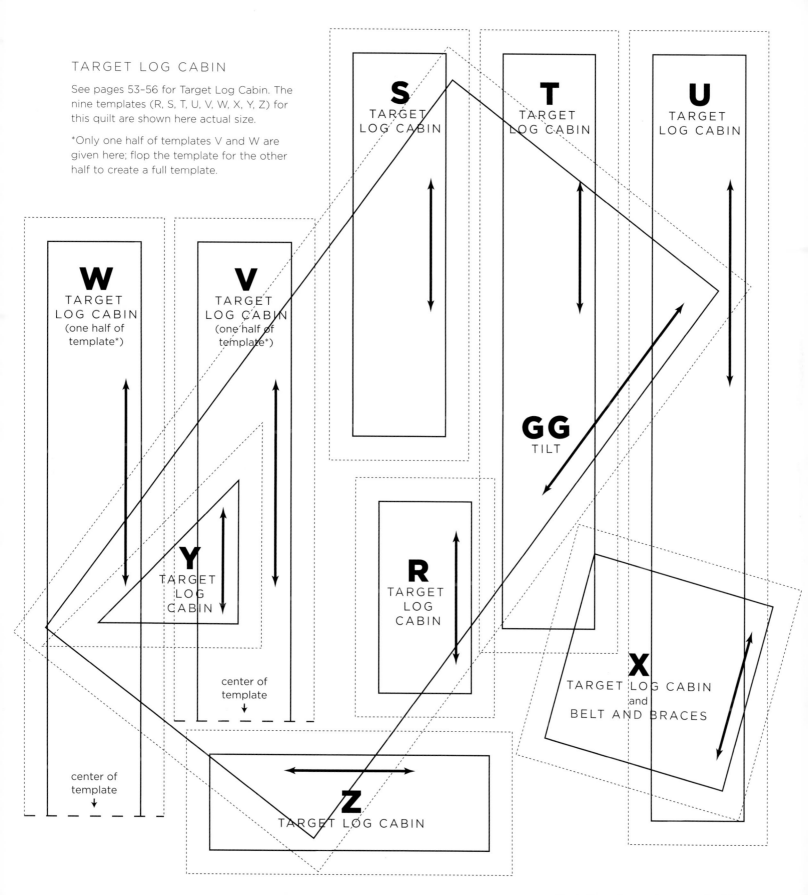

TARGET LOG CABIN

See pages 53-56 for Target Log Cabin. The nine templates (R, S, T, U, V, W, X, Y, Z) for this quilt are shown here actual size.

*Only one half of templates V and W are given here; flop the template for the other half to create a full template.

S
TARGET
LOG CABIN

T
TARGET
LOG CABIN

U
TARGET
LOG CABIN

W
TARGET
LOG CABIN
(one half of
template*)

V
TARGET
LOG CABIN
(one half of
template*)

GG
TILT

Y
TARGET
LOG
CABIN

R
TARGET
LOG
CABIN

center of
template ↓

X
TARGET LOG CABIN
and
BELT AND BRACES

center of
template ↓

Z
TARGET LOG CABIN

HAZE KILIM

See pages 70–74 for Haze Kilim. The four templates (F, G, H, J) for this quilt are shown here (and on the next page) actual size. The stripes on the fabrics should run in the same direction as the grain-line marker (the arrow) next to the quilt name (the other arrow is for Earthy Mitered Boxes).

*Only one half of template F is given here; flop the template for the other half to create a full template.

**Flop templates G and J for G reverse and J reverse. It is important to use reverse G and reverse J where indicated in the instructions so the stripes run in the correct direction.

DAMASK QUARTERS

See pages 134–137 for Damask Quarters. The two templates (K, L) for this quilt are shown here actual size.

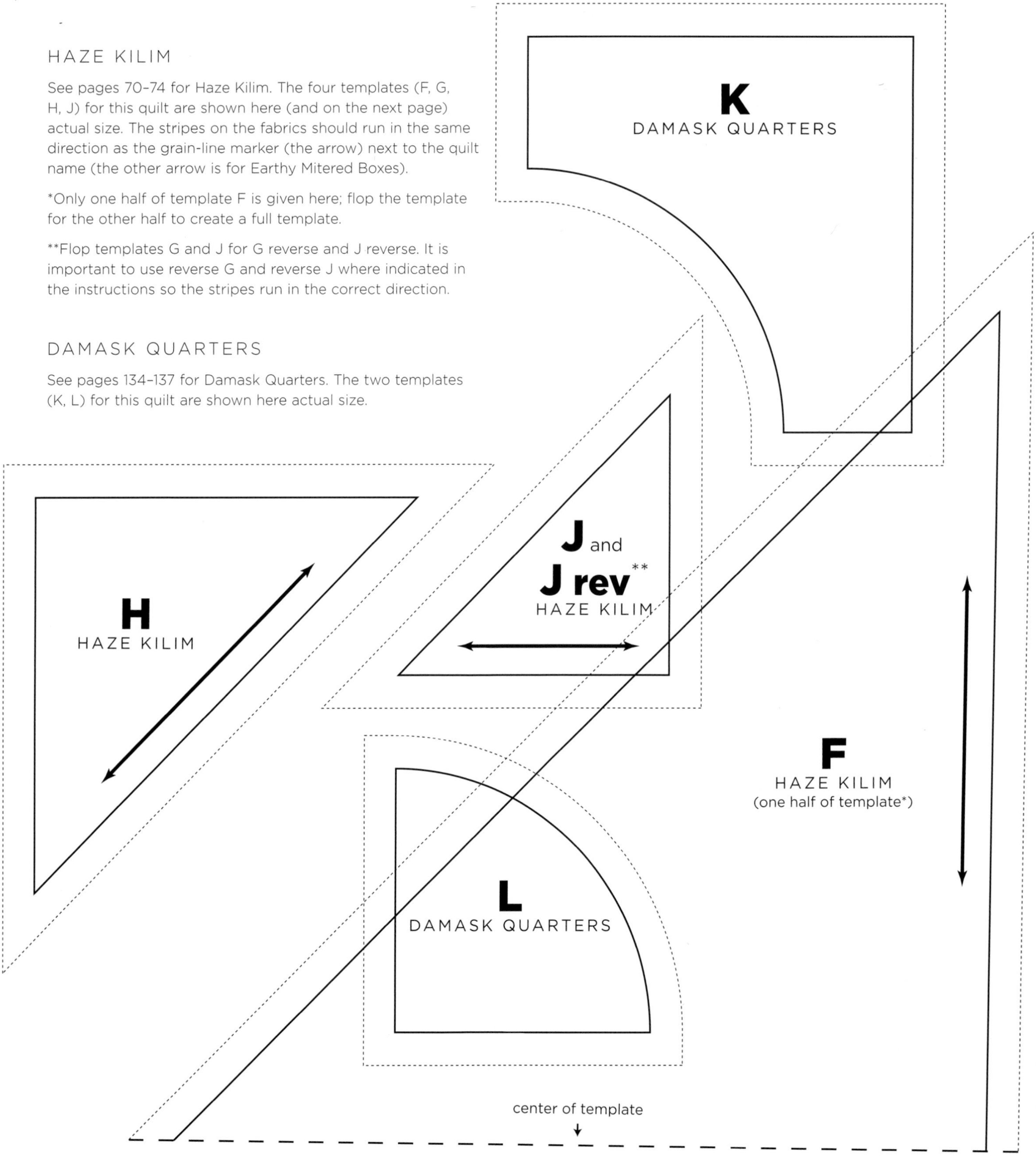

K
DAMASK QUARTERS

H
HAZE KILIM

J and
J rev**
HAZE KILIM

F
HAZE KILIM
(one half of template*)

L
DAMASK QUARTERS

center of template

CLAY TILES and INDIGO POINTS

See pages 75–77 for Clay Tiles and pages 78–81 for Indigo Points. The templates (A, B) for these patchworks are shown here actual size.

EARTHY MITERED BOXES

See pages 82–85 for Earthy Mitered Boxes. The three templates (LL, MM, G) for this quilt are shown here actual size. The stripes on the fabrics should run in the same direction as the grain-line marker (the arrow). Be sure to use the grain-line marker (the arrow) next to the quilt name on template G (the other arrow is for Haze Kilim).

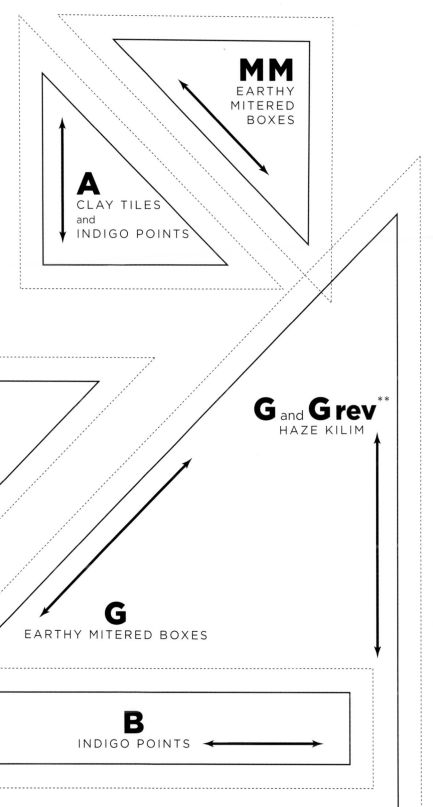

MM
EARTHY
MITERED
BOXES

A
CLAY TILES
and
INDIGO POINTS

G and **G** rev**
HAZE KILIM

LL
EARTHY MITERED BOXES

G
EARTHY MITERED BOXES

B
INDIGO POINTS

CIRCLE OF STARS

See pages 98–105 for Circle of Stars. The four templates (H, J, K, L) for this quilt are shown here (and on the next page) actual size.

*Only one half of template L is given here; flop the template for the other half to create a full template.

BORDERED DIAMONDS

See pages 116–119 for Bordered Diamonds. The diamond template (Z) for this quilt is shown here actual size.

*Only one half of template Z is given here; flop the template for the other half to create a full template.

**Use this grain line if the fabric print is nondirectional; if the print is upright, ignore the arrow and fussy-cut the diamond with the flowers upright inside the shape.

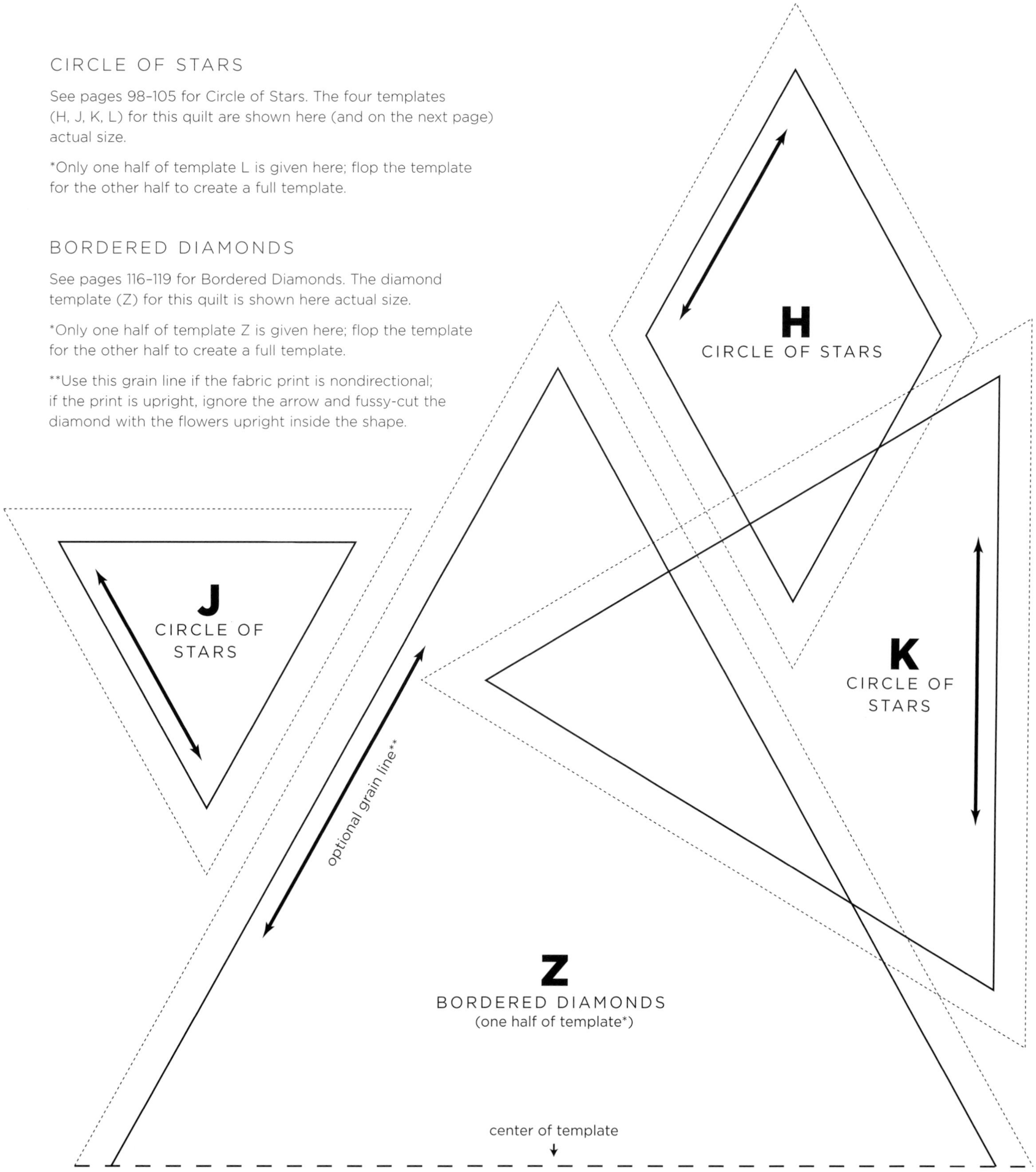

H
CIRCLE OF STARS

J
CIRCLE OF STARS

K
CIRCLE OF STARS

optional grain line**

Z
BORDERED DIAMONDS
(one half of template*)

center of template

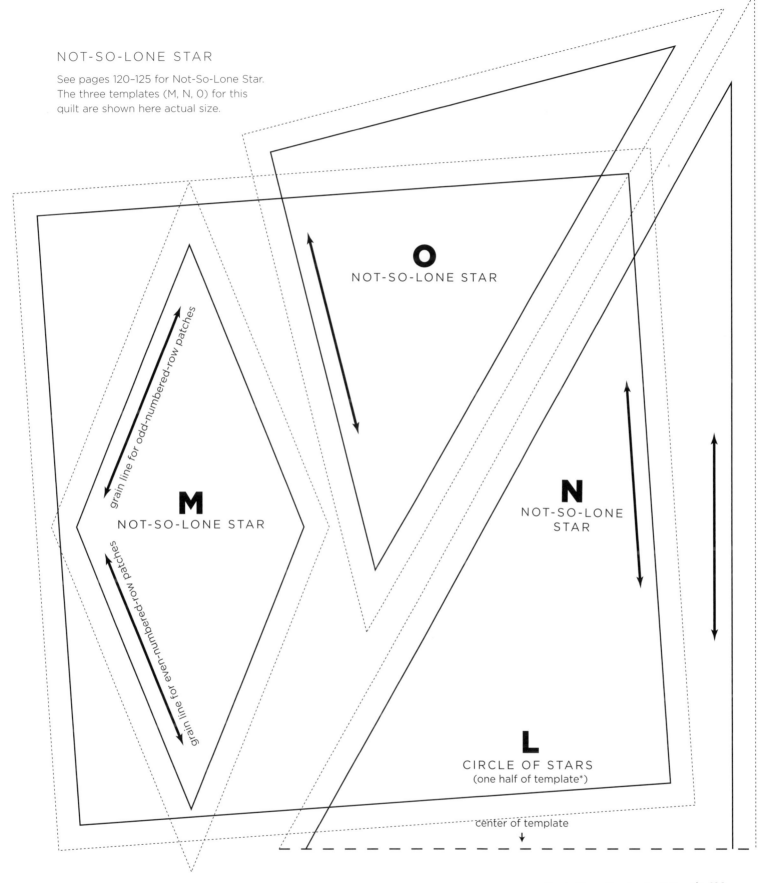

NOT-SO-LONE STAR

See pages 120–125 for Not-So-Lone Star.
The three templates (M, N, O) for this
quilt are shown here actual size.

O

NOT-SO-LONE STAR

grain line for odd-numbered-row patches

M

NOT-SO-LONE STAR

grain line for even-numbered-row patches

N

NOT-SO-LONE
STAR

L

CIRCLE OF STARS
(one half of template*)

center of template

ST. MARKS

See pages 111–115 for St. Marks. The four templates (A, B, C, D) for this quilt are shown here reduced to 80 percent. Enlarge them all to 125 percent on a photocopier for the actual-size templates.

*Only one half of templates B and C are given here; flop the template for the other half to create a full template.

**Flop template D for D reverse.

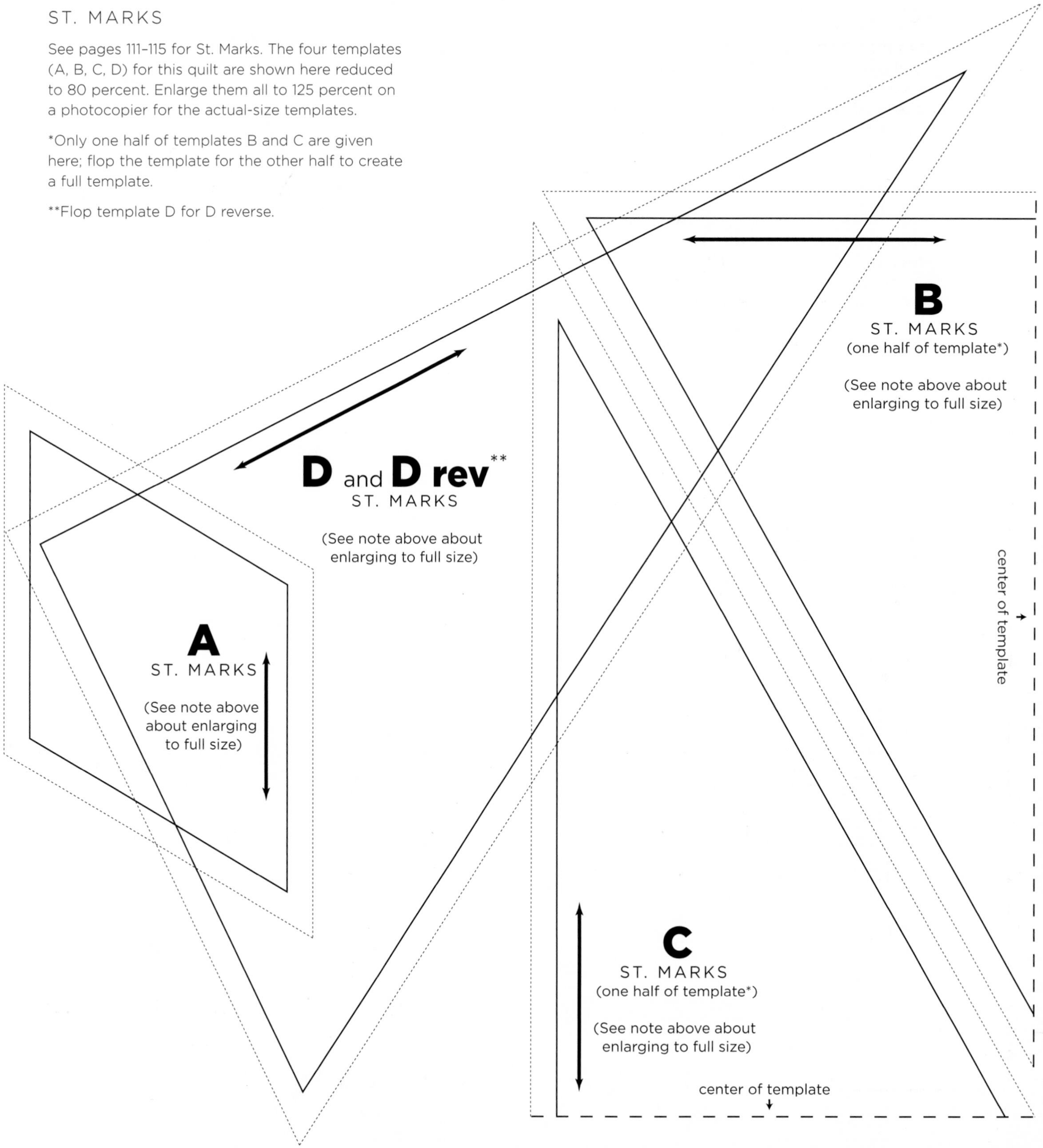

B

ST. MARKS
(one half of template*)

(See note above about enlarging to full size)

D and **D rev****
ST. MARKS

(See note above about enlarging to full size)

center of template

A
ST. MARKS

(See note above about enlarging to full size)

C
ST. MARKS
(one half of template*)

(See note above about enlarging to full size)

center of template

BICYCLE WHEEL

See pages 172–177 for Bicycle Wheel. The two templates (S, T) for this quilt are shown here reduced to 80 percent. Enlarge them both to 125 percent on a photocopier for the actual-size templates. The actual-size template S can then be photocopied and cut out for the 20 paper foundation pieces needed to make the rims on the bicycle wheels.

BELT AND BRACES

See pages 50–52 for Belt and Braces. Three of the templates for this quilt are shown here actual size (E, F, G). The remaining template—template X—used for this quilt is also used for Target Log Cabin (see page 185).

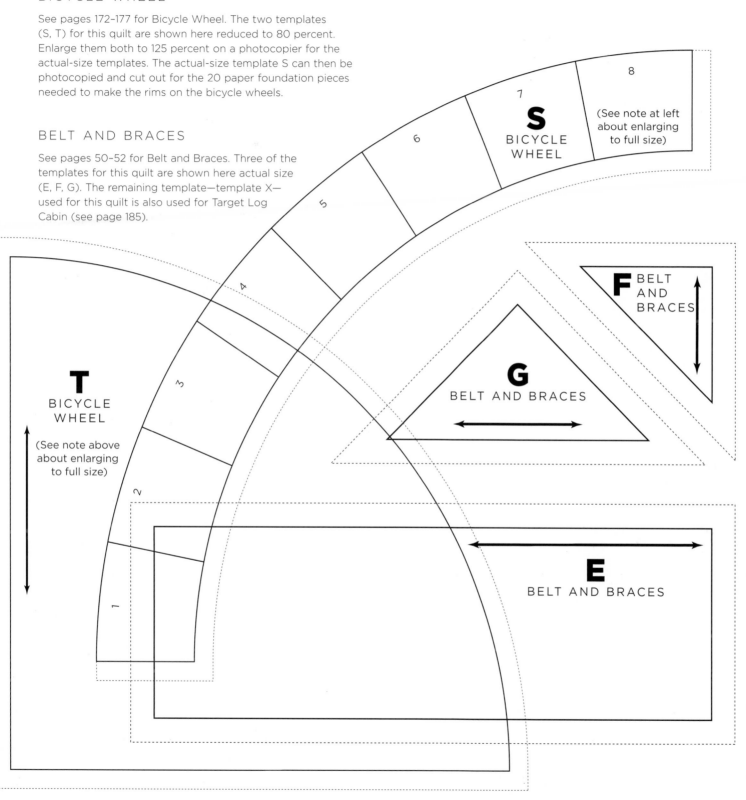

ACKNOWLEDGMENTS

Biggest thank-yous are to Judy Irish for her glorious quilting and to Debbie Patterson for her glorious photography.

Thanks also to Donna Laing for quilting. Thanks to Bekah Lynch, Pauline Smith, Claudia Chaback, and Katy Kingston for sewing patchwork tops so beautifully.

Thanks to Judy Baldwin, Sally Davis, Corienne Kramer, Kathy Merrick, Bobbi Penniman, and Julie Stockler for keeping things running at Glorious Color and for pitching in whenever Kaffe arrived at Liza's house and turned it into an atelier.

Thanks to Drew, Alex, and Elizabeth Lucy for their encouragement and help with sewing, cutting, cooking, and photography.

For their generosity, we thank the people at Wrights for notions, Coats for thread, Westminster Fibers for fabric, Pat LaPierre for the Free Motion Slider, and Alicia's Attic for Clearview Triangles.

Thanks to Sally Harding, who keeps us all on schedule and refines every word and number. To Melanie Falick, who has jumped into publishing patchwork with enthusiasm. To Anna Christian, our book designer, who got the point of our aesthetic so perfectly.

Thanks also to Katy Kingston for her creative flair and help, and to Richard Womersley for his support.

Biggest thanks to Brandon Mably for endless inspiration and support throughout the making of this book.

PHOTO CREDITS

All photographs copyright © Debbie Patterson unless listed below:

All photographs of flat quilts shown with instructions copyright © Jon Stewart

PAGE 6 Top row: Left (Kaffe Fassett Studio); Center (Shutterstock) / 2nd Row: Center (Shutterstock), Right (Kaffe Fassett Studio) / 3rd Row: Center (Kaffe Fassett Studio). PAGE 9 Shutterstock. PAGE 10 Top Row: Left and Right (Kaffe Fassett Studio); Center (Shutterstock) / 2nd Row: Left and Right (Kaffe Fassett Studio), Center (Shutterstock) / 3rd Row: Left and Center (Kaffe Fassett Studio), Right (Shutterstock). PAGE 11 Top Row: Left and Center (Kaffe Fassett Studio); Right (Shutterstock) / 2nd Row: Left and Right (Kaffe Fassett Studio); Center (Shutterstock) / 3rd Row: All (Shutterstock). PAGE 12 Both Photos: Kaffe Fassett Studio. PAGE 28 Shutterstock. PAGE 32 Both Photos: Kaffe Fassett Studio. PAGE 36 Top Row: All Shutterstock / 2nd Row: Left and Right (Shutterstock); Center (Kaffe Fassett Studio) / 3rd Row: Left and Right (Kaffe Fassett Studio); Center (Shutterstock). PAGE 37 Top Row: Left (Kaffe Fassett Studio); Center and Right (Shutterstock) / 2nd Row: Left and Right (Kaffe Fassett Studio): Center (Shutterstock) / 3rd Row: Left and Center (Shutterstock); Right (Kaffe Fassett Studio). PAGE 38 Top (Shutterstock). PAGE 52 Both Photos (Shutterstock). PAGE 58 Top (Kaffe Fassett Studio); Center and Bottom (Shutterstock). PAGE 62 Top Row: Left and Center (Kaffe Fassett Studio); Right (Shutterstock) / 2nd Row Left and Center (Kaffe Fassett Studio); Right (Shutterstock); 3rd Row: All (Shutterstock). PAGE 63 Top Row: Left (Kaffe Fassett Studio); Center and Right (Shutterstock) / 2nd Row: Left (Shutterstock); Center and Right (Kaffe Fassett Studio) / 3rd Row: Left (Shutterstock); Center and Right: Kaffe Fassett Studio. PAGE 64 Top (Kaffe Fassett Studio). PAGE 65 Kaffe Fassett Studio. PAGE 72 Kaffe Fassett Studio. PAGE 80 Both Photos (Kaffe Fassett Studio). PAGE 84 Kaffe Fassett Studio. PAGE 86 Top Row: Left (Kaffe Fassett Studio); Center and Right (Shutterstock) / Center Row: Left and Right (Shutterstock); Center: Kaffe Fassett Studio / Bottom Row: Left (Shutterstock); Right (Kaffe Fassett Studio). PAGE 87 Top Row: Left (Kaffe Fassett Studio); Center and Right (Shutterstock) / Center Row: Left and Center: Shutterstock; Right (Kaffe Fassett Studio) / 3rd Row: Left and Right (Kaffe Fassett Studio); Center (Shutterstock). PAGE 88 Top (Kaffe Fassett Studio). PAGE 89 Kaffe Fassett Studio. PAGE 102 Kaffe Fassett Studio. PAGE 108 Kaffe Fassett Studio. PAGE 112 Kaffe Fassett Studio. PAGE 119 Top (Shutterstock); Bottom (Kaffe Fassett Studio). PAGE 126 Top Row: Left (Shutterstock); Right (Kaffe Fassett Studio) / 2nd Row: Left and Right (Kaffe Fassett Studio); Center (Shutterstock) / 3rd Row: All (Shutterstock). PAGE 127 Top Row: Left and Right (Shutterstock); Center (Kaffe Fassett Studio) / 2nd Row: All (Shutterstock) 3rd Row: Left and Center (Kaffe Fassett Studio); Right (Shutterstock). PAGE 128 Bottom (Kaffe Fassett Studio). PAGE 129 Bottom (Shutterstock). PAGE 136 Top (Shutterstock); Bottom (Kaffe Fassett Studio). PAGE 140 Top (Shutterstock). PAGE 143 Kaffe Fassett Studio. PAGE 146 Both Photos (Shutterstock). PAGE 148 Top Row: All Photos (Shutterstock) / 2nd Row: Left and Center (Shutterstock); Right (Kaffe Fassett Studio) / 3rd Row: Left and Right: Shutterstock; Center: Kaffe Fassett Studio. PAGE 149 Top Row: Left and Right (Kaffe Fassett Studio); Center (Shutterstock) / 2nd Row: Left and Center (Kaffe Fassett Studio); Right (Shutterstock) / 3rd Row: Left and Center (Kaffe Fassett Studio); Right (Shutterstock). PAGE 150 Top (Kaffe Fassett Studio). PAGE 151 Kaffe Fassett Studio. PAGE 161 Shutterstock. PAGE 168 Both Photos (Kaffe Fassett Studio). PAGE 174 Both Photos (Kaffe Fassett Studio).